Road Trip EAST

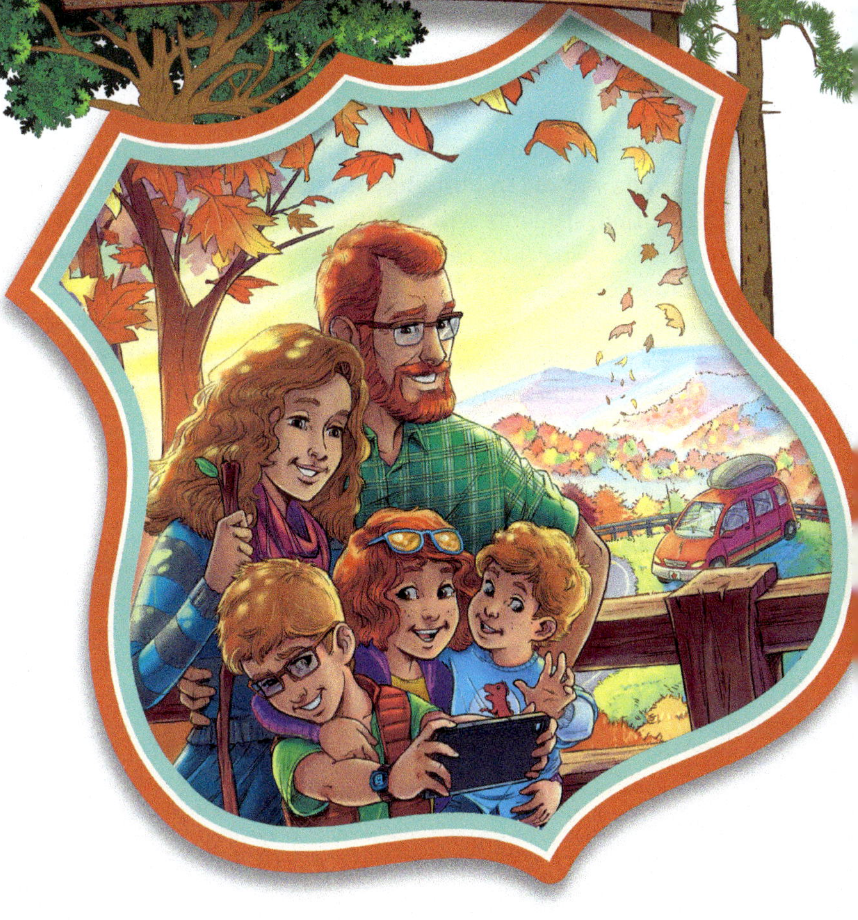

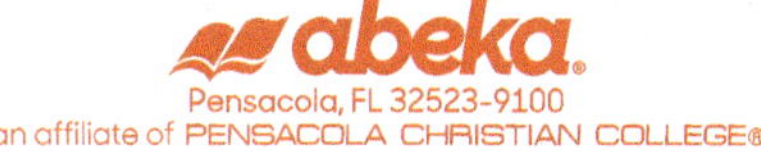

abeka®
Pensacola, FL 32523-9100
an affiliate of PENSACOLA CHRISTIAN COLLEGE®

Explore four **unique** regions, visit *historic* landmarks, and meet famous people **EAST** of the Mississippi with the Jackson family on their

To Teachers and Parents

Whether hiking through the Allegheny National Forest in Pennsylvania or visiting the 9/11 Memorial in New York City, students are in for an exciting adventure in *Road Trip East*. As they travel the four regions east of the Mississippi River, students will appreciate classic poetry by Robert Frost and illustrations by Robert Lawson, explore geographical landscapes and historical monuments, and delight in heartwarming historical fiction and nonfiction narratives. A variety of selections will aid in building knowledge of literary concepts. In addition, students will analyze elements of poetry such as *repetition*, *meter*, and *rhyme scheme* as well as the *compare-contrast text structure*. Students will begin to recognize, analyze, and write selections that compare and contrast two topics. Throughout the reading of this book students will be challenged to analyze the material and draw conclusions from it with thinking questions marked with an asterisk.

Road Trip East

Staff Credits
Managing Editor: Amy Yohe
Product Manager: Tanya Harrington
Edition Editors: Tanya Harrington, Juliane Roberts, Tammy Collins, Rachel Grosnick, Savannah Patrick, Cheryl Reid, Kayla Sanders, Bethany Urbina
Designer: Ruth Ann Chappell
Cover Illustrator: Joshua Burylo
Illustrators: Brian Jekel, Joshua Burylo, Peter Kothe, Jamieson Jekel, Jeremy Gorman, Sarah Fragela, Dakotah Black, Bobby Dalrymple

Credits appear on p. 200, which is considered an extension of copyright page.

Cataloging Data
Road trip east -- 1st ed.
200 p. : col. ill. ; 22 cm
1. Readers (Elementary) 2. Reading (Elementary)
III. Abeka Book, Inc.
Library of Congress: PE 1119 .R63 2020
Dewey System: 428.6

Contents

Welcome to New England:

On the Road *Bethany Urbina* 1

Each Has Something Good *Author Unknown* 4

New England 5

Robert Frost *Kayla Sanders* 6

BUILD ON IT–Rhyme 9

The Last Word of a Bluebird *Robert Frost* 9

Now Close the Windows *Robert Frost* 11

The Pasture *Robert Frost* 12

After-Apple Picking *Robert Frost* 13

BUILD ON IT–Descriptive Text Structure 16

Take Me Out to the Ball Game *Kayla Sanders* . . . 16

The Middle Bear *Eleanor Estes* 20

BUILD ON IT–Sequential Text Structure 36

Robert Lawson *Kayla Sanders* 36

Little Georgie Sings a Song *Robert Lawson* 39

Welcome to the Mid-Atlantic:

Lost in the Forest *Bethany Urbina* 50

Mid-Atlantic 54

BUILD ON IT–Repetition 55

The Barn-Swallow *William Sargent* 55

BUILD ON IT–Meter and Rhyme Scheme 56

The Wind *Robert Louis Stevenson* 58

The President's Train Ride 60

BUILD ON IT–Biography 64

A Light in the Darkness *Donna M. Covey* 65

cont.

The Best of All *Fanny Crosby* **75**

Near the Cross *Fanny Crosby* **76**

Never Forget *Savannah Patrick* **77**

The Tower of Voices *Kayla Sanders* **84**

The Old Flag *H. C. Bunner* **86**

Ringing in the Fourth of July
Carolyn Sherwin Bailey **88**

God Bless Our Native Land
Charles T. Brooks and John S. Dwight **98**

Daniel and the Lions' Den *Daniel 6* **99**

Welcome to the Southeast:

A Home-Cooked Meal *Bethany Urbina* **106**

Southeast **110**

BUILD ON IT—Compare and Contrast Text Structure . . . **111**

Sweet Treats *Kayla Sanders* **114**

Elizabeth Irvine's Ride *Author Unknown* **117**

cont.

Chimney Rock Park *Kayla Sanders* **124**
Wilma Rudolph *Cheryl Reid* **128**
Daniel Boone's Daughter *Aileen Fisher* **132**

Welcome to the Great Lakes:

A Great Camping Trip *Bethany Urbina* **144**
Great Lakes **149**
"That's a crackerjack!" **150**
Caramel-Coated Popcorn Recipe **151**
Bill's Bill *Harry Stephen Keeler* **152**
A Friend in Sable *Savannah Patrick* **167**
Little Gray Shoes *Arleta Richardson* **176**
Which Is Which? *Kayla Sanders* **183**
Jesus—Our Lighthouse *Kayla Sanders* **187**
The Little Road *Nancy Byrd Turner* **190**
BUILD ON IT—Review Activities **192**

Pronunciation Key

Symbol	Example	Symbol	Example
ā	āte	ŏ	nŏt
â	dâre	oi	boil
ă	făt	o͞o	fo͞od
ä	fäther	o͝o	bo͝ok
ə	ago (ə·gō′)	ou	out
ē	ēven	th	thin
ĕ	ĕgg	t̶h̶	t̶h̶ere
ẽ (ər)	pondẽr	tū	pictūre
ī	īce	ū	ūnit
ĭ	ĭt	û	hûrt
ō	ōver	ŭ	ŭp
ô	côrd, taught, saw	zh	measure

On the Road

Bethany Urbina

The last car door had been closed. The last seat belt had been fastened. Christy and Caleb looked at their parents, then at each other. Everyone had sparkling eyes and huge smiles. Even little Cole was bouncing in his car seat. The day was finally here! Today the Jackson family would begin their road trip through the eastern United States of America. Mom and Dad had visited the United States many times before; after all, it was only a few hours from their home in Canada, but this would be the first time for any of the children. Caleb began to flip through his book of American National Parks while Christy gazed at the beautiful pictures of American cities in her travel magazine. Cole was just as content with his tiny book of farm animals since it played music and made animal noises.

"Where are we going first, Dad?" asked Caleb as the car pulled out onto the main road.

"We are going to start in the corner of the country that is closest to us," Dad replied, "with Maine, New Hampshire, Vermont, Massachusetts, Connecticut, and Rhode Island. This area is called New England."

Mom jumped in to explain. "This corner of the country was controlled by England for many years until the American colonists gained their independence," she said. "Back then it was not fifty states, only thirteen colonies. Many of those colonies make up New England today."

"That's part of what makes New England, and the states surrounding it, a very special place to visit. Many of the houses and buildings from the early days of America's history are still standing there today," Dad added.

As the trip went on, Mom and Dad told them about the rocky coast of Maine, the busy city of Boston, and the picture-perfect countryside that covered New England. In a few short hours, Christy and Caleb began to see it for themselves. The beautiful green land rolled like a scene from a storybook. White clapboard houses began to appear in the distance, many paired with large red barns. Little Cole began to kick his feet and point out the window.

"Mommy! Horse!" he said again and again as his eyes fixed on a pasture dotted with copper colored mares. Cole shouted out each animal he saw as it passed, but Christy and Caleb hardly noticed him. Seeing the sights in person was so much better than looking at pictures in books. They couldn't look away. The longer they drove, the more excited they became to see all that this "New England" had to offer.

Think About It!

Give the correct answer.

1. Where was the Jackson family from?

2. Which members of the Jackson family had visited the United States before?

*3. What would the Jackson family *not* see while exploring New England?

a. animals
b. buildings from early days
c. desert plains
d. historical sights
e. Iowa farmland
f. old red barns
g. rocky coast of Maine

*Thinking questions are marked with an asterisk.

WELCOME
to
MAINE

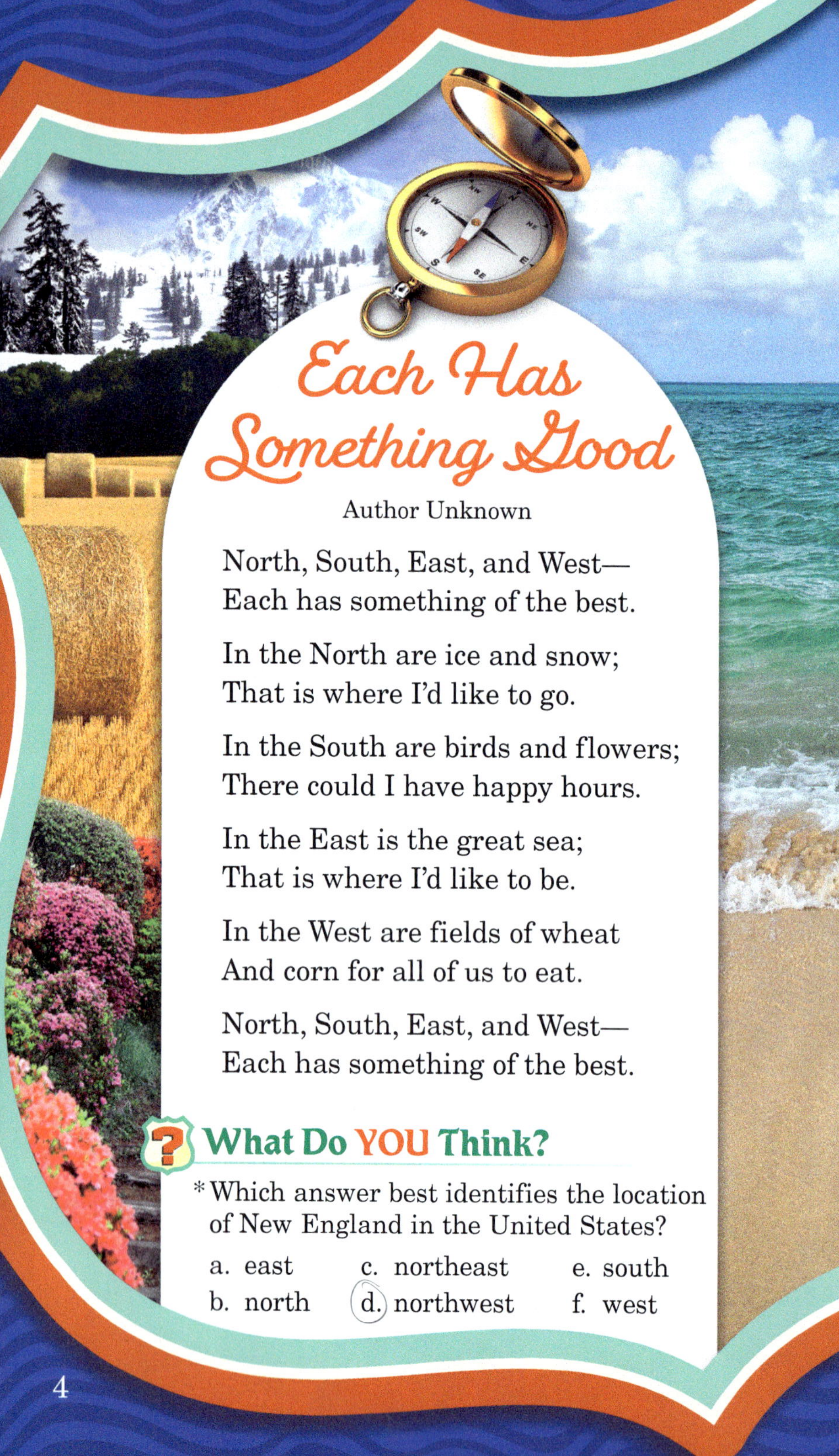

Each Has Something Good

Author Unknown

North, South, East, and West—
Each has something of the best.

In the North are ice and snow;
That is where I'd like to go.

In the South are birds and flowers;
There could I have happy hours.

In the East is the great sea;
That is where I'd like to be.

In the West are fields of wheat
And corn for all of us to eat.

North, South, East, and West—
Each has something of the best.

? What Do YOU Think?

* Which answer best identifies the location of New England in the United States?

a. east
b. north
c. northeast
d. northwest
e. south
f. west

Eastern United States

New England

Let's travel with the Jackson family as they explore the United States east of the Mississippi River. Their *Road Trip East* will prove to be an exciting adventure for all of us as we discover famous authors, classic stories, beautiful landscapes, and interesting landmarks.

Come along for the ride!

Maine

Along the way, you might spot a Peregrine falcon in Acadia National Park, Maine.

Acadia National Park

Robert Frost

Kayla Sanders

Little Robert Frost was born in 1874 out west in San Francisco. Robert's father, William, was a rising journalist who wrote exciting news articles of the day. In 1885, when William died, Robert and his family moved east to Massachusetts. There Robert finished high school, and Robert's mother taught school.

Although Robert's father had been a writer and his mother a teacher, Robert didn't begin writing poetry until after he was married and working a dairy farm in New Hampshire.

Robert tried to get his poetry published in America, but he had no success. Then in 1912, Robert moved his family to England, and his poetry career blossomed. He published his first book of poetry, *A Boy's Will*, and soon a second book followed, called *North of Boston*.

Two years later, he returned to the United States with his family and published four more books of poetry. Soon, he won the Pulitzer Prize, the highest award achieved by any writer. After Robert Frost won *four* Pulitzer Prizes, President John F. Kennedy awarded him the Congressional Gold Medal for his influence in America.

Robert Frost still influences readers through his poems about farm life in New Hampshire, harsh winters in Vermont, and apple picking in Massachusetts. The way he wrote about boys climbing trees and wandering in the woodlands paints beautiful pictures in the minds of readers and listeners.

As we read Robert Frost's poetry, notice the descriptive details he uses to make you feel like you're really in New England.

Think About It!

Give the correct answer.

1. True/False: Robert Frost wrote poetry when he lived in San Francisco. Explain why your answer makes sense.

*2. Inference is using clues plus what you already know to figure out something. How old was Robert Frost when he moved to New England? Underline the clues that support your answer.

*3. List three things that may have influenced Robert Frost's poetry.

inference—*thinking logically through the facts given to reach a conclusion*

You will find the world's longest candy counter, measuring over 100 feet long, at Chutters in Littleton, New Hampshire. The Jackson family may enjoy a tasty treat from this longstanding establishment.

BUILD ON IT

Rhyme

Rhyme is the repetition of similar sounds and may be found anywhere, but it most often comes at the end of a line in poetry. Rhyme may be found at the end of multiple lines in a row, or it may be found in alternating lines. What pattern will you find in "The Last Word of a Bluebird"?

The Last Word of a Bluebird

Robert Frost
As told to a child

As I went out a Crow
In a low voice said, "Oh,
I was looking for you.
How do you do?
I just came to tell you
To tell Lesley (will you?)
That her little Bluebird
Wanted me to bring word
That the north wind last night
That made the stars bright
And made ice on the trough
Almost made him cough
His tail feathers off.

He just had to fly!
But he sent her Good-by,
And said to be good,
And wear her red hood,
And look for skunk tracks
In the snow with an ax—
And do everything!
And perhaps in the spring
He would come back and sing."

Think About It!

Give the correct answer.

1. Draw lines to match the rhyming words from "The Last Word of a Bluebird."

bluebird	bright	everything	ax
crow	cough	fly	good-by
night	do	good	hood
trough	oh	tracks	sing
you	off		spring
	word		

2. Does the pattern for rhyming words in this poem alternate with each line, or is it found in multiple lines in a row?

*3. In what time of year would the events of this poem most likely take place? How do you know?

*4. What is the main idea in "The Last Word of a Bluebird"?

Questions marked with a building block highlight fourth grade literary concepts.

To BUILD ON IT, see page 192.

Now Close the Windows

Robert Frost

Now close the windows and hush all the fields:
    If the trees must, let them silently toss;
No bird is singing now, and if there is,
    Be it my loss.

It will be long ere[1] the marshes[2] resume,[3]
    It will be long ere the earliest bird:
So close the windows and not hear the wind,
    But see all wind-stirred.

---

[1] ere—*before*
[2] marsh—*an area of low land that becomes flooded during rainy season*
[3] resume—*begin again after a time*

Think About It!

Give the correct answer.

* How does the title emphasize the main idea?

The Pasture

Robert Frost

I'm going out to clean the pasture spring;
I'll only stop to rake the leaves away
(And wait to watch the water clear, I may):
I shan't be gone long.—You come too.

I'm going out to fetch the little calf
That's standing by the mother. It's so young
It totters when she licks it with her tongue.
I shan't be gone long.—You come too.

Think About It!

Give the correct answer.

*1. How many stanzas are in "The Pasture"?

*2. In which stanza does the narrator ask the reader to go to the pasture?

After Apple-Picking

Robert Frost

My long two-pointed ladder's sticking through a tree
Toward heaven still,
And there's a barrel that I didn't fill
Beside it, and there may be two or three
Apples I didn't pick upon some bough.
But I am done with apple-picking now.
Essence of winter sleep is on the night,
The scent of apples: I am drowsing off.
I cannot rub the strangeness from my sight
I got from looking through a pane of glass
I skimmed this morning from the drinking trough
And held against the world of hoary[1] grass.

[1] hoary—*gray or white*

It melted, and I let it fall and break.
But I was well
Upon my way to sleep before it fell,
And I could tell
What form my dreaming was about to take.
Magnified apples appear and disappear,
Stem end and blossom end,
And every fleck of russet[2] showing clear.
My instep arch not only keeps the ache,
It keeps the pressure of a ladder-round.
I feel the ladder sway as the boughs bend.
And I keep hearing from the cellar bin
The rumbling sound
Of load on load of apples coming in.
For I have had too much
Of apple-picking: I am overtired
Of the great harvest I myself desired.
There were ten thousand thousand fruit to touch,
Cherish in hand, lift down, and not let fall.
For all
That struck the earth,
No matter if not bruised or spiked with stubble,

[2]fleck of russet—*spot of brown*

Went surely to the cider-apple heap
As of no worth.
One can see what will trouble
This sleep of mine, whatever sleep it is.
Were he not gone,
The woodchuck could say whether it's like his
Long sleep, as I describe its coming on,
Or just some human sleep.

Think About It!

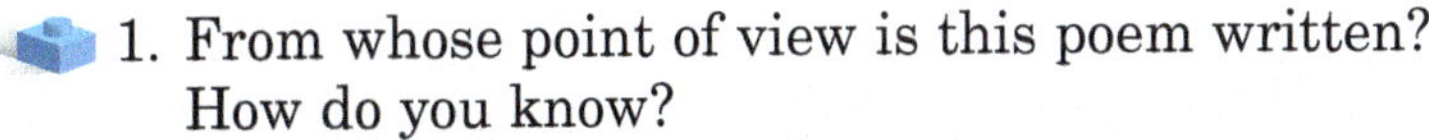

Give the correct answer.

1. From whose point of view is this poem written? How do you know?

*2. Robert Frost uses four out of the five senses to vividly describe the poem's setting. Underline descriptive phrases he uses to communicate what he sees, smells, hears, and feels.

What Do YOU Think?

How do you think the narrator felt about a season of apple picking?

Massachusetts

Fenway Park, Boston

After apple picking in the country-side, the Jacksons head to Fenway Park in Boston, Massachusetts, to enjoy one of the nation's favorite pastimes—baseball.

BUILD ON IT

Descriptive Text Structure

Remember that an author has a purpose in mind when writing. A descriptive text structure is used when an author wants to write an informative selection to describe a topic. The author's description is usually based on one or more of the five senses. See what senses are used to describe the atmosphere at Fenway Park.

Take Me Out to the Ball Game

Kayla Sanders

It's game day at Fenway Park. Before the game begins, arrive in your team gear, wander the surrounding area, and enjoy the historic atmosphere, street vendors, and street performers. Grab a hot dog and some popcorn. Take a picture with the memorial statues. Stroll down Jersey Street to see the championship banners and the row of

informative—*nonfiction selection for the purpose of providing information*

retired jersey numbers of baseball legends. Walk through the concourse, decorated with brick and Fenway-green walls and concession stands, and finally step into the stadium.

Baseball is considered to be America's favorite pastime, or activity. You can visit many famous baseball parks around the United States like Yankee Stadium in New York or Wrigley Field in Chicago. However, none can compare to Fenway Park, home of the Boston Red Sox.

Built in 1912, Fenway Park is the oldest stadium currently in use in America today. In 2012, the park celebrated its 100th birthday and was registered as a national and historical landmark. Over the past century, Fenway has seen many changes. People from all over the world come to see the baseball park and its famous features.

One well-known feature of Fenway Park is the lone red seat. In 1946, legendary Ted Williams hit the longest homerun Fenway Park had ever seen at that time. The stray baseball landed in Section 42, Row 37, Seat 21. The ball had traveled over 500 feet. This distance equals more than the length of an entire football field! To remember this historic moment, the Boston Red Sox painted Seat 21 bright red while the surrounding seats remained green.

The most famous feature of Fenway Park is the Green Monster. The Green Monster is the large green wall located behind left field. The wall was originally built to prevent people without tickets from watching the game from across the street. Today, the same wall stands at 37 feet tall! That's about as tall as the telephone pole outside your house. In 2003, over 250 seats were added on the top of the Green Monster's roof to allow an action-packed, ultimate fan experience. If you want a view like none other during a baseball game, this is the best place to sit.

Inside the Green Monster, a manual scoreboard was installed, which is still used today. A person must sit inside the Green Monster and update the score by hand. If you take a tour of Fenway Park, you can go inside the Green Monster to see how the scoreboard works during ball games.

Speaking of the scoreboard, it looks like we've hit the seventh-inning stretch here at Fenway. Do you know what that means? It's time to stand tall, stretch, and proudly sing our favorite baseball song: "Take Me Out to the Ball Game!"

Think About It!

Give the correct answer.

*1. Why do you think Fenway Park was registered as a historical landmark?

2. Name something you can see, smell, hear, or taste in or around the stadium.

3. What text structure did the author use to write this selection? Explain your answer.

4. Why is Section 42, Row 37, Seat 21 painted red?

5. What is the Green Monster?

Original Fenway Park

The Middle Bear

Eleanor Estes

Each year the American Library Association awards Newbery honors to authors of remarkable children's books written the previous year. In 1941, Eleanor Estes was honored for her book entitled *The Middle Moffat.*

The Moffat books retell the memories of the author growing up in New Haven, Connecticut, when it was a small town. Let's step back in time and watch what happens as this little town prepares for an important event.

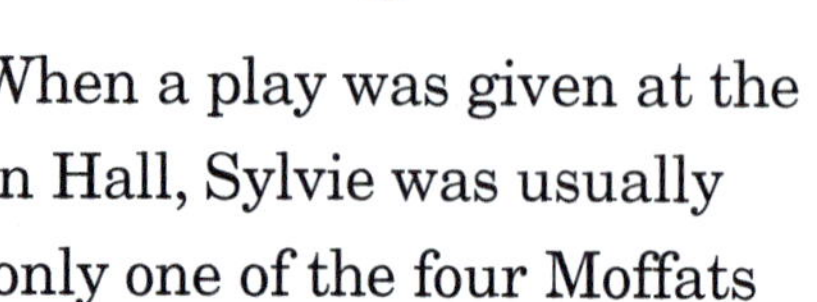

When a play was given at the Town Hall, Sylvie was usually the only one of the four Moffats who was in it. However, once in a while the others were in a play. For instance, Rufus had been the smallest of the seven dwarfs. And once Janey had been a

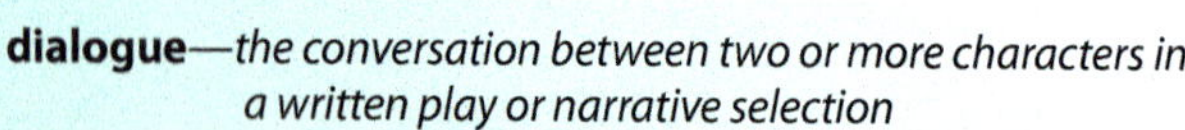

dialogue—*the conversation between two or more characters in a written play or narrative selection*

butterfly. She had not been an altogether successful butterfly, though, for she had tripped on the sole of her stocking, turning a somersault all across the stage. And whereas Joey was rarely in a play, he was often in charge of switching the lights on and off.

Now there was to be a play at the Town Hall, *The Three Bears*, and all four of the Moffats were going to be in it. Miss Chichester,[1] the school teacher, was putting it on. But the money for the tickets was not going into her pocket or into the Moffats' pocket, even though they were all in the play. The money was to help pay for the new parish house.[2] The old one had burned down last May and now a new one was being built. *The Three Bears* was to help raise the money to finish it. A benefit performance, it was called.

In this benefit performance, Sylvie was to play the part of Goldilocks. Joey was to be the big bear, Rufus the little bear, and Janey the middle bear. Jane had not asked to be the middle bear. It just naturally came out that way. The middle Moffat was going to be the middle bear.

As a rule, Joey did not enjoy the idea of acting in a play any more than he liked going to school. However, he felt this play would be different. He felt it would be like having a disguise on, to be inside of a bear costume. And Jane felt the same

---

[1] Chichester (chĭ′chĕs·tẽr)

[2] parish house—*a church building used for socials, business, and other activities*

way. She thought the people in the audience would not recognize her as the butterfly who turned a somersault across the stage, because she would be comfortably hidden inside her brown bear costume. As for Rufus, he hoped that Sylvie, the Goldilocks of this game, would not sit down too hard on that nice little chair of his and really break it to bits. It was such a good chair, and he wished he had it at home.

Mama was making all the costumes, even the bear heads. A big one for Joey, a little one for Rufus, and a middle-sized one for Jane. Of course, she wasn't making them out of bear fur; she was using brown outing flannel.

Now Jane was trying on her middle bear costume. She stepped into the body of the costume, and then Mama put the head on her.

"Make the holes for the eyes big enough," Jane begged. "So I'll see where I'm going and won't turn somersaults."

"Well," said Mama, "if I cut the eyes any larger you will look like a deep-sea diver instead of a bear."

"Oh, well . . ." said Jane hastily. "A bear's got to look like a bear. Never mind making them any bigger, then."

Besides being in the play, each of the Moffats also had ten tickets to sell. And since Rufus really was too little to go from house to house and street to street selling tickets, the other three Moffats had even more to dispose of. Forty tickets!

The tickets were very hard to sell. But little by little the pile did dwindle.[3] If only everybody were like Mrs. Stokes, they would go very fast. She bought four tickets! Jane was embarrassed.

"Tell your mother she doesn't have to buy all those tickets just 'cause all of us are in the play," she instructed Nancy.

But all the Stokeses insisted they really wanted to go. And even if none of the Moffats were in it, they would still want to go, for the play would help to build a new parish house. *What nice people!* thought Jane. Here they were, a family who went to the white clapboard church, buying tickets to help build a parish house for Janey's church. She hoped she would be a good middle bear, so they would be proud they knew her.

At last it was the night of the play. The four Moffats knew their lines perfectly. This was not

[3] dwindle—*become smaller*

surprising, considering they all lived in the same house and could practice their lines any time they wanted to. And, besides this, they had had two rehearsals, one in regular clothes and one in their bear costumes.

When Jane reached the Town Hall, she was surprised to find there were many features on the program besides *The Three Bears*. The Gillespie twins were going to give a piano duet. "By the Brook," it was called. A boy was going to play the violin. And Miss Beale was going to sing a song. A big program. And the Moffats, all of them except Mama, were going to watch this whole performance from behind the scenes. They could not sit in the audience with the regular people with their bear costumes on, for that would give the whole show away.

Sylvie was busy putting makeup on herself and on some others' faces. Jane watched them enviously. The only trouble with wearing a bear costume, she thought, was that she couldn't have her face painted. Well, she quickly consoled herself, she certainly would not have stage fright inside her bear head. Whereas she might if there were just paint on her face. "Somebody has been sitting in my chair," she rehearsed her lines. She stepped into her bear costume. But before putting on her head, she helped Rufus into his bear uniform. He didn't call it a costume. A uniform. A bear uniform.

Jane set his head on his shoulders, found his two eyes for him so he could see out, and the little bear was ready.

Joey had no difficulty stepping into his costume and even in finding his own two eyes. Now the big bear and the little bear were ready. Jane looked around for her head, to put it on. Where was it?

"Where's my head?" she asked. "My bear head."

Nobody paid any attention to her. Miss Chichester was running back and forth and all around, giving an order here and an order there. Once as she rushed by, causing a great breeze, Jane yelled to make herself heard, "How can we act *The Three Bears* unless I find my middle bear head?"

"Not just now. I'm too busy" was all Miss Chichester said.

Everybody was too busy to help Jane find her head. Sylvie was helping someone else dress. Joey was busy running around doing this and doing that for Miss Chichester. And the little old janitor was busy tightening ropes and making sure the lights were working. Rufus could not be torn from a hole in the curtain. He was looking for Mama.

Jane sighed. *Everybody's busy,* she thought.

Goodness, thought Jane. *The curtain will go up, and the middle bear won't be a whole bear.* This was worse than tripping over her stocking the time she was a butterfly. Maybe Joey and Rufus somehow or another had two heads on. They didn't, though, just their own. Phew, it was warm inside these bear costumes. Jane stood beside Rufus and looked through another small hole in the curtain. Oh! The big door was open! People were beginning to arrive. And what kind of a bear would she be without a head? Maybe she wouldn't be allowed to be a bear at all. But there certainly could not be three bears without a middle one.

"Don't worry," said Rufus, not moving an inch from his spot. "Lend you mine for half the play . . ."

"Thanks," said Jane. "But we all have to have our heads on all through the whole thing."

The Stokeses were coming in! Jane felt worried. The only person who might be able to fix a new bear head for her in a hurry was Mama. Oh, if she had only made a couple of spare heads. But Mama wasn't coming yet. Jane resolved[4] to go and meet her.

She ran all the way home. But the house was dark. Mama had already left. And she must have gone around the other way or Jane would have passed her. Jane raced back to the Town Hall. There! Now! The lights were dim. The entertainment had begun. Jane tried to open the side door. Chief Mulligan was guarding this entrance. He did

[4] resolved—*made a firm decision*

not want to let her in at first. He thought she was just a person. But when she showed him her costume, he opened the door just wide enough for her. The bear costume was as good as a password.

Jane tiptoed up the three steps and went backstage, wondering what would happen now. The show always goes on. There was some comfort in that thought. Somehow, someone would fix her head. Or possibly while she was gone her middle bear head had been found. She hoped she would not have to act with her head bare.

Miss Chichester snatched her.

"Oh, there you are, Jane! Hop into your costume, dear."

"I'm in it," said Jane. "But I can't find my middle bear head."

"What else will go wrong?" said Miss Chichester, grasping her own head.

Jane looked at her in surprise. What else *had* gone wrong? Had others lost worse than their heads?

"Where's the janitor?" Miss Chichester asked. "Maybe he let his grandchildren borrow it."

Jane knew he hadn't, but she couldn't tell Miss Chichester for she had already flown off. And then Janey had an idea.

"I know what," she said to Joey. "Pin me together." And she pulled the neck part of her costume up over her head. Joey pinned it with two safety pins, and he cut two holes for her eyes. This costume was not comfortable now. Pulling it up and pinning it this way lifted Jane's arms so she had trouble making them hang down the way she thought a bear's should. However, at any rate, she now had a bear head of sorts.

"Do I look like a bear?" she asked Rufus.

"Don't you worry," said Sylvie, coming up. "You look like a very nice little animal."

"But I'm supposed to be a bear, not a nice little animal," said Jane.

"Well," said Sylvie, "people will know you are supposed to be a bear because Rufus and Joey both have their bear heads on."

So Jane resigned[5] herself to not being a perfect bear. She tried to comfort herself with the thought that she would still be in disguise. She hoped her acting would be so good it would counterbalance[6] her bad head. "Somebody has been eating my porridge," she practiced.

Miss Chichester appeared. "The janitor said no," she said. She thoughtfully surveyed Jane a moment. "Hm-m-m, a makeshift,"[7] she observed. "Well, it's better than nothing," she agreed with Jane. But she decided to switch the order of the program around in order to give everybody one last chance to find the middle bear's real head.

[5] resign—*submit to or accept circumstances*
[6] counterbalance—*offset; make up for*
[7] makeshift—*last-minute arrangement*

She sent Miss Beale out onto the stage. Everybody hoped that while Miss Beale was singing "In an Old-Fashioned Garden," the head would appear. But it didn't.

"Keep a little in the background," said Miss Chichester to Jane. "Perhaps people will not notice."

If I can only see where the background is, thought Jane. For she found it even harder to keep her eyes close to the holes cut in her costume than it had been to the real ones in her regular bear head.

Now the heavy curtain rolled up. It didn't stick halfway up as it sometimes did, and Sylvie, Goldilocks, in a blue pinafore and socks, ran out onto the stage amid loud applause. The play had begun! Sylvie had a great deal of acting to do all by herself before the three bears came home. But she wasn't scared. She was used to being on the stage alone.

Jane's heart pounded as she and Joey and Rufus waited for their cue to come home. If only she didn't trip and turn a somersault, for she really could not see very well. Somehow she managed to see out of only one eye at a time. These eyeholes must have been cut crooked. One hole kept getting hooked on her nose.

"Now!" Miss Chichester whispered. "Cue! Out with you three bears."

Joe, Jane, and Rufus, the three bears, lumbered[8] out onto the stage. They were never supposed to just walk, always lumber and lope.[9]

The applause was tremendous. It startled the three bears. The Town Hall was packed. Somebody must have sold a lot of tickets.

"There's Mama," said Rufus. He said it out loud.

He wasn't supposed to say anything out loud except about his porridge, his chair, and his bed. But anyway he said, "There's Mama." Jane could not see Mama. Lumbering out onto the stage had dislocated her costume so that now she could not see at all. Fortunately the footlights shone through the brown flannel of her costume so she could keep away from the edge of the stage and not fall off.

The Moffats all knew their lines so well they did not forget them once. The only trouble was they did not have much chance to say them because the applause was so great every time they opened their mouths. At last, however, they reached the act about the three beds. An extra platform had been set up on the stage to look like the upstairs of a three bears' house. The three bears lumbered slowly up the steps.

Suddenly shouts arose all over the Hall:

"Her head! Her head! The middle bear's head!"

---

[8]lumber—*move heavily and clumsily*

[9]lope—*move along with a swinging stride*

"Sh-sh-sh," said others. "See what's going to happen."

As Jane could not see very well she had no idea what these shouts referred to. She had the same head on now that she had had on all during this play so far. Why then all these shouts? Or had she really stayed in the background the way Miss Chichester had asked her to, and the audience had only just discovered about the makeshift?

"Oh," whispered Joey to Jane. "I see it. It's your real bear head and it's on the top of my bedpost."

"O-o-o-h!" said Jane. "Get it down."

"How can I?" said Joe. "With all these people watching me?"

"Try and get it when you punch your bed," urged Jane.

Joey was examining his big bear's bed now. "Hm-m-m," he said fiercely. "Somebody has been lying on my bed . . ." But he couldn't reach the middle bear's head. He did try. But he couldn't quite reach it, and there was more laughter from the audience.

Jane pulled her costume about until she could see through the eyehole. Ah, there was her head! On the post of the big bear's bed. No wonder people were laughing. What a place for the middle bear's head. Here she was, without it. And there it was, without her. Jane resolved to get it. Somehow or other she would rescue her head before this play was completely over. Now was her chance. It was her turn to talk about her bed. Instead, Jane said:

"Somebody has been trying on my head, and there it is!"

Jane hopped up on Joey's bed. She grabbed her middle bear head.

"Yes," she repeated. "Somebody has been trying on my head," but as she added, "and here it is!" the safety pins that held her makeshift head together popped open. The audience burst into roars of laughter as Janey's own real head emerged. Only for a second though. For she clapped her middle bear head right on as fast as she could, and hopped off the bed. *Goodness,* she thought, *I showed my real face and I didn't have any paint on it.*

Unfortunately Jane still could not see, for she had stuck her bear head on backward. But the audience loved it. They clapped and they stamped. "Bravo! Bravo! Bravo, middle bear!" Big boys at the back of the hall put their fingers in their mouths and whistled. And it was a long, long time before Jane could say:

"Somebody has been sleeping in my bed," and the play could go on. At last Rufus discovered Goldilocks in his little bed, and she leaped out of the window. That was the end of the play, and the curtain rolled down.

When the bowing began, Miss Chichester tried to send Jane in backward, thinking the back of her was the front of her. Fortunately, Rufus held Jane by one

paw, and Joey held the other. So she didn't get lost. And the three bears lumbered dizzily on and off many times, sometimes with Sylvie, and sometimes alone. And somebody yelled for "The mysterious middle bear!"

Miss Chichester turned Jane's head around for this bow, and at last Jane really did look like a perfect middle bear. Furthermore, she could see out. There was Mama, laughing so hard the tears were rolling down her cheeks. And there was Nancy Stokes with all the Stokeses. Jane bowed and lumbered off the stage. She felt good now. Acting was fun, she thought, especially if you could be disguised in a bear uniform. And this time she had not turned a somersault across the stage as she had the time she was a butterfly. True, she had lost her head. But she had found it. And the show had gone on, the way people say shows always do.

Moreover, the Moffats had nice warm bear pajamas to sleep in for the rest of the winter. Of course they didn't go to bed with the bear heads on. But the rest of the costumes were nice and warm.

Think About It!

Give the correct answer.

1. What is the purpose of this narrative?
   a. to entertain the reader with a story
   b. to inform the reader about how to perform a play
2. This narrative structure includes _____.
   a. characters   b. plot   c. rhyme
   d. setting   e. stanzas

*3. Who is the main character? Explain your answer.

4. What problem did the main character have?

*5. What was the solution to the main character's problem? Was it successful?

*6. What was the middle bear's clever reaction to finding her head?

What Do YOU Think?

* Do you think the play was more of a success because of the incident or would it have been better if everything had gone smoothly?

If you enjoy plays and musicals, you will find this next stop fascinating. In New Haven, Connecticut, there is a museum of musical instruments from all around the world—some over 2,000 years old!

To BUILD ON IT, see page 193.

BUILD ON IT

Sequential Text Structure

Remember that an author has a purpose in mind when writing. If an author wants to write an informative selection he may use a sequential text structure. This type of text structure is used to retell the events of something in the order that they happened or to inform the reader of how to follow a step-by-step process. See if you can discover which type of sequential selection was used in writing about Robert Lawson's life.

Robert Lawson

Kayla Sanders

Robert Lawson was born in New York City in early October 1892. Growing up, he lived in the small town of Montclair, New Jersey. Robert discovered he had a talent for drawing, and after high school, he moved back to New York City to study art.

Robert's art was first published in a magazine in 1914 before he went to fight in World War I. After the war ended in 1918, Robert picked up his pen again. He illustrated his first children's book in 1922 for author George Randolph Chester.

New York City

Over the years, Robert illustrated many other children's books, such as *The Story of Ferdinand* and *Mr. Popper's Penguins*.

Finally, Robert decided to write and illustrate his own children's book. As he wrote, Robert loved using the technique of telling a story about a main character through the eyes of another character. In 1939, he published *Ben and Me*. This was a story about young Benjamin Franklin but told by his mouse, Amos.

Then in 1941, Robert won an award called the Caldecott Medal for his book *They Were Strong and Good*. This award is given to the illustrator of the best picture book of the year.

Not long after, Robert won the Newbery Medal for writing the most extraordinary children's book of the year. This award-winning book, set in Westport, Connecticut, was called *Rabbit Hill*. The story

Westport, Connecticut

is about a family of rabbits adjusting to a new way of life with new neighbors. Robert used animals to tell a story about what was happening to people in real life after World War II. At the time, everyone was trying to figure out how to go back to life as it was before the war began. You will enjoy the next selection, "Little Georgie Sings a Song," a chapter excerpt from *Rabbit Hill*.

excerpt—*a short selection from a book*

Think It Through

Give the correct answer.

1. Does this sequential selection retell events or inform the reader of a step-by-step process?
2. Underline the signal words used to identify the story's structure.
3. Number these events of Robert's life in sequential order.

   __1__ He fought in World War I.

   __3__ The Newbery Medal was awarded to Robert for *Rabbit Hill*.

   __2__ Robert moved back to his birthplace and studied at an art school.

   __5__ Robert illustrated his first children's book.

   __4__ He began to write and illustrate his own children's book.

4. Why would it not make sense for event 4 to come after event 5?

Little Georgie Sings a Song

Robert Lawson

New folks are coming to live in the big house on Rabbit Hill, and to the animals that brings the hope of a good garden and good eating. No one is more excited than Little Georgie Rabbit, who is sent to tell Uncle Analdas[1] the news, in spite of his mother's uneasiness about him going alone.

It was barely daylight when Little Georgie started his journey. In spite of her worrying, Mother had managed to put up a small but nourishing[2] lunch. This, along with a letter to Uncle Analdas, was packed in a little knapsack and slung over his shoulder. Father went along as far as the Twin Bridges. As they stepped briskly down the

[1] Analdas (ə·năl′dŭs)
[2] nourishing—*healthy*

Hill, the whole valley was a lake of mist on which rounded treetops swam like floating islands. From old orchards rose a mounting chorus as the birds greeted the new day. Mothers chirped and chuckled and scolded as they swept and tidied the nests. On the topmost branches, their menfolk warbled and shrilled and mocked one another.

The houses were all asleep, even the Dogs of the Man-at-the-Crossroads were quiet, but the Little Animals were up and about. They met the Gray Fox returning from a night up Weston way. He looked footsore and sleepy, and a few chicken feathers still clung to his ruff.[3] The Red Buck trotted daintily across the Black Road to wish them good luck and good morning, but Father, for once, had no time for long social conversation. This was business, and no Rabbit in the county knew his business any better than Father—few as well.

"Now, son," he said firmly, "your mother is in a very nervous state, and you are not to add to her worries by taking unnecessary risks or by carelessness. No dawdling[4] and no foolishness. Keep close to the road but well off it. Watch your bridges and your crossings. What do you do when you come to a bridge?"

"I hide well," answered Georgie, "and wait a good long time. I look all around for Dogs. I look up the road for cars and down the road for cars. When

[3] ruff—*fur around the neck*
[4] dawdling—*wasting time*

everything's clear, I run across—fast. I hide again and look around to be sure I've not been seen. Then I go on. The same thing for crossings."

"Good," said Father. "Now recite your Dogs."

Little Georgie closed his eyes and dutifully recited, "Man-at-the-Crossroads: two Mongrels;[5] Good Hill Road: Dalmatian; house on Long Hill: Collie, noisy, no wind; Norfield Church corner: Police Dog, no nose; On the High Ridge, red farm-house: Bulldog and Setter, don't bother; farmhouse with the big barns: Old Hound, very dangerous . . ." and so on. He recited every dog on the route clear up to Danbury way. He did it without a mistake and swelled with pride at Father's approving nod.

"Excellent," said Father. "Now do you remember your checks and doublings?"[6] Little Georgie closed his eyes again and rattled off, quite fast, "Sharp right and double left, double left and double right, dead stop and back flip, right jump, left jump, false trip, and briar dive."

"Splendid," said Father. "Now attend[7] carefully. Size up your Dog; don't waste speed on a plodder, you may need it later. If he's a rusher, check, double, and freeze. Your freeze, by the way, is still rather bad. You have a tendency to flick your left ear; you must watch that. The High Ridge is very open country so keep in the shadow of the stone

[5] mongrel—*dog of mixed breed*
[6] checks and doublings—*sudden stops and sharp turns*
[7] attend—*pay close attention to*

walls and mark the earth piles. Porkey has lots of relatives along there, and if you are pressed hard, any of them will gladly take you in. Just tell them who you are, and don't forget to thank them. After a chase, hide up and take at least ten minutes' rest. And if you have to *really* run, tighten that knapsack strap, lace back your ears, put your stomach to the ground, and RUN!

"Get along with you now, and mind—no foolishness. We shall expect you and Uncle Analdas by tomorrow evening at the latest."

Little Georgie crossed the Twin Bridges in perfect form, returned Father's approving wave, and was off on his own.

It was gray and misty as he crossed Good Hill Road, and the Dalmatian still slept. So, apparently, did the Collie up the road, for all was quiet as he plodded up Long Hill. People were beginning to stir as he approached Norfield Church corner; little plumes[8] of blue smoke were rising from kitchen chimneys, and the air was pleasant with the smell of frying bacon.

As he expected, the Police Dog rushed him there, but he wasted little time on that affair. Loping along with tantalizing[9] slowness until they were almost on an old fallen apple tree buried in briars, he executed[10] a dead stop, a right jump,

[8]plumes—*clouds resembling feathers*
[9]tantalizing—*teasing*
[10]execute—*carry out; do*

and a freeze. The bellowing brute over-ran him and plunged headlong into the thorny tangle. His agonized howls were sweet music to Little Georgie as he hopped sedately[11] along toward the High Ridge. He wished Father had been there to see how skillfully he had worked and to note that during the freeze his left ear hadn't flickered once.

The sun was well up when he emerged on the High Ridge. On the porch of the red farmhouse, the Bulldog and the Setter slept soundly, soaking up its warmth. On any other occasion, Little Georgie would have been tempted to wake them to enjoy their silly efforts at running, but, mindful of Father's instructions, he kept dutifully on his way.

The High Ridge was a long and open strip of country, very uninteresting to Little Georgie. The

[11] sedately—*quietly; calmly*

view, over miles and miles of rolling woods and meadows, was very beautiful, but he didn't care especially about views. The brilliant blue sky and the bright little cream-puff clouds were beautiful too. They made him feel good; so did the warm sun, but frankly he was becoming slightly bored. So, to ease his boredom, he began to make a little song.

The words had been rattling around in his head for some days now, and the music was there too, but he couldn't quite get them straight and fitted together. So he hummed and he sang and he whistled. He tried the words this way and that way; he stopped and started and changed the notes around. Finally, he got the first line so that it suited him. So Georgie sang that line over and over again to be sure that he wouldn't forget it when he started on the second line.

It must have been this preoccupation[12] with his song that made Little Georgie careless and almost led to his undoing. He scarcely noticed that he had passed the house with the big barns, and he was just starting to sing his first line for the forty-seventh time when there came the roaring rush of the Old Hound right on his heels, so close that he could feel the hot breath.

Instinctively,[13] Little Georgie made several wild springs that carried him temporarily out of harm's way. He paused a fraction of a second to tighten

[12]preoccupation—*distraction*

[13]instinctively—*naturally, without having to think*

the knapsack strap and then set off at a good steady pace. "Don't waste speed on a plodder" was Father's rule. He tried a few checks and doubles and circlings, although he knew they were pretty useless. The great fields were too bare, and the Old Hound knew all the tricks. No matter how he turned and dodged, the Hound was always there, coming along at his heavy gallop. He looked for Woodchuck burrows, but there were none in sight. "Well, I guess I'll have to run it out," said Little Georgie.

He pulled the knapsack strap tighter, laced back his ears, put his stomach to the ground, and RAN. And *how* he ran!

The warm sun had loosened his muscles; the air was invigorating.[14] Little Georgie's leaps grew longer and longer. Never had he felt so young and strong. His legs were like coiled springs of steel that released themselves of their own accord. He was hardly conscious of any effort, only of his hind feet pounding the ground. Each time they hit, those wonderful springs released and shot him through the air. He sailed over fences and stone walls as though they were mole runs. Why, this was almost like flying! Now he understood what Zip the Swallow had been driving at when he tried to describe what it was like. He glanced back at the Old Hound, far behind now, but still coming along at his plodding gallop. He was old and must be tiring, while he, Little Georgie, felt stronger and

[14] invigorate—*fill with energy*

more vigorous at every leap. Why didn't the old fool give up and go home?

And then, as he shot over the brow of a slight rise, he suddenly knew. *He had forgotten Deadman's Brook!* There it lay before him, broad and deep, curving out in a great silvery loop. He, the son of Father, gentleman hunter from the Bluegrass, had been driven into a trap, a trap that even Porkey should have been able to avoid! Whether he turned to right or left, the loop of the creek hemmed him in, and the Old Hound could easily cut him off. There was nothing for it but to jump!

This sickening realization had not reduced his speed; now he redoubled it. The slope helped, and his soaring leaps became prodigious.[15] The wind whistled through his laced-back ears. Still he kept his head, as Father would have wished him to. He picked a spot where the bank was high and firm; he spaced his jumps so they would come out exactly right.

The take-off was perfect. He put every ounce of leg muscle into that final kick and sailed out into

[15] prodigious—*great; enormous*

space. Below him, he could see the cream-puff clouds mirrored in the dark water. He could see the pebbles on the bottom and the silver flash of frightened minnows dashing away from his flying shadow. Then, with a breath-taking thump, he landed, turned seven somersaults, and came up sitting in a clump of soft lush grass.

He froze, motionless except for heaving sides, and watched the Old Hound come thundering down the slope, slide to a stop and, after eyeing the water disgustedly, take his way slowly homeward, his dripping tongue almost dragging the ground.

Little Georgie did not need to remember Father's rule for a ten-minute rest after a good run. He was blown and he knew it, but he did remember his lunch, so he unstrapped the little knapsack and combined lunch and rest. He had been really scared for a moment, but as his wind came back and his lunch went down, his spirits came up.

Father would be angry, and rightly, for he had made two mistakes: he had let himself be surprised, and he had run right into a dangerous trap. But that leap! Never in the history of the county had any rabbit jumped Deadman's Brook, not even Father. He marked the exact spot and calculated the width of the stream there—at least eighteen feet! And with his rising spirits, the words and the notes of his song suddenly tumbled into place.

Little Georgie lay back in the warm grass and sang his song—

New Folks coming, oh my!
New Folks coming, oh my!
New Folks coming, oh my!
Oh my! Oh my!

Think About It!

Give the correct answer.

1. What type of story is "Little Georgie Sings a Song?" Circle your answer(s) in the chart below. Explain your answer.

Text Structures	
Narrative	**Informative**—nonfiction
Fiction	Descriptive
Nonfiction	Sequential

2. What was the purpose of Georgie's adventure?
3. What was the main reason for the excitement of the new folks coming?
4. Why was it so important that Georgie knew all the details about the dogs?

*5. Is the title "Little Georgie Sings a Song" of any importance to the story?

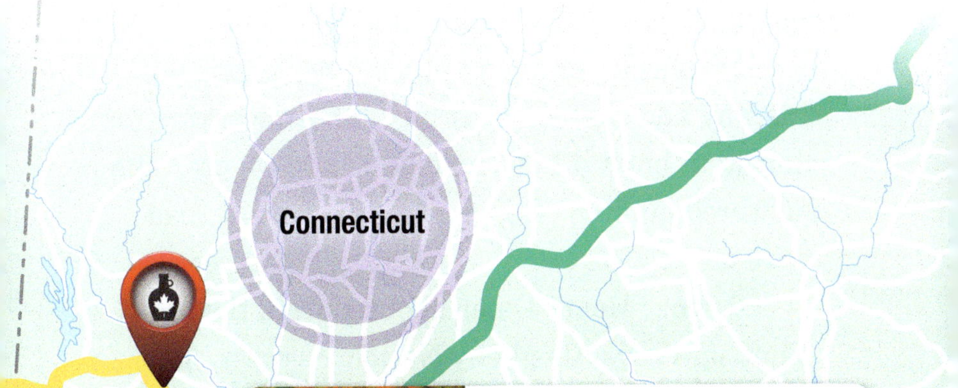

Connecticut

MAPLE SYRUP FOR SALE AT FARM HOUSE

Before we leave the New England countryside, let's pull into a family farm to buy some maple syrup—one of the Jacksons' favorite things.

To BUILD ON IT, see page 194.

Lost in the Forest

Bethany Urbina

The little van rolled along, winding its way through the mountains. Christy and Caleb were so busy reading in the back seat that they didn't realize how worried Mom and Dad were becoming. Up in the front seat Dad whispered, "Does your cellphone have any satellite signal yet?"

Mom shook her head and held her phone out this way and that way. "It hasn't been working for almost an hour. I have no idea where we are," she answered quietly. "Do we even know what road we're on?"

"Oh look, Mom!" Caleb shouted from the back. "That sign says Allegheny National Forest. There's a chapter about it right here in my book."

Christy peered over his shoulder. "It says Allegheny National Forest is in northwestern Pennsylvania."

Dad gave Mom a secret smile in the front seat and whispered, “I’m so glad our children love to read.”

“There’s a ranger station up ahead!” said Mom. “Maybe the ranger can tell us where to go.”

The little van slowed to a stop in front of a tiny cabin, where a man in uniform was waiting. He waved and walked toward the van.

“How can I help you folks?” he asked kindly.

“We seem to have lost our way,” Dad admitted, shrugging his shoulders. “We’re heading towards New York, then Philadelphia.”

“You aren’t too lost yet,” the ranger chuckled. “Let me grab you folks a map!” The ranger pulled a map from his bag and opened it for Dad, pointing to a patch of green. “You are here at the national forest. If you head north on this road here, you should make it there before sunset without a problem.”

"Thank you, sir," replied Dad gratefully. "You see, we don't come this way very often."

"We're from Canada," added Mom. "We started off on a road trip to show our children the United States."

"Well, welcome to the U.S.A!" the ranger said, shaking hands with everyone. "Do you kids like learning about history?" Caleb quickly nodded his head, and the ranger continued, "You'll love this part of the country. It's overflowing with history! There's Independence Hall and the Liberty Bell in Philadelphia; national monuments in Washington, D.C.; colonial villages in Virginia; and the famous fort of Boonesborough in Kentucky."

Caleb and Christy's eyes grew wide. "Can we visit all those places, Dad?" Christy asked.

"We can surely try, Christy!" Dad smiled and once again turned to the ranger. "Thank you so much for your help."

"It's my pleasure!" he called back as the van pulled away. "Enjoy your American road trip!"

Think About It!

Give the correct answer.

*1. Why was Dad glad that his children loved to read?

*2. How did the ranger help the Jackson family?

*3. Of all the places that the ranger described, which would you be most excited to visit?

Mid-Atlantic

Let's travel through the historic mid-Atlantic region with the Jacksons. We'll uncover famous landmarks, national monuments, unique wildlife, and even read about a remarkable letter written to a famous president.

But first, let's take a look around the Allegheny National Forest.

Allegheny National Forest

Independence Hall

9/11 Memorial

Mid-Atlantic

Allegheny National Forest

Hiking through the Allegheny National Forest, you might spot the American woodcock more often referred to as the timberdoodle.

BUILD ON IT

Repetition

Sometimes lines, phrases, and even stanzas are repeated in poetry. This is called repetition. The poet uses repetition when he wants to draw your attention to something important. Underline the lines of the poem that demonstrate repetition.

The Barn-Swallow

William Sargent

In the Allegheny Mountains
When the apple orchards bloom
I know of eaves in a big red barn
Where I'll find nesting room.

I'm coming back! I'm coming back!
My wings are on the wind;
I'm coming back with the spring-time
To the hills I've left behind.

I'm coming back! I'm coming back!
To the hills that I know best,
Where the mountains sleep, and the winds walk,
And where my wings can rest.

Meter and Rhyme Scheme

Much like a song, many poems have a definite rhythm or **meter**. Meter is a pattern made by stressed and unstressed syllables in a poem. This pattern creates the flowing musical quality for which poetry is well known. Each meter is composed of a small group of stressed and unstressed syllables.

Many, but not all, poems rhyme. **Rhyme scheme** is the pattern that rhyming words make at the end of the lines of a poem. Poets use different rhyme schemes. Rhymes may be found in multiple lines in a row or in alternating lines. We use *a*, *b*, *c*, and so on, to mark the pattern at the end of the line. Lines that rhyme share the same letter.

Think It Through

Give the correct answer.

1. What do we call repeated lines, phrases, or stanzas in a poem?
2. The pattern of unstressed and stressed syllables in a poem is called ______.

   a. meter b. rhyme c. rhyme scheme
3. How do we mark rhyme scheme in a poem?
4. Read the poem on page 57 aloud. Reread the poem aloud, clapping once for each syllable. Listen for the pattern of the meter as you clap.

Each Has Something Good

Author Unknown

North, South, East, and West— a
Each has something of the best. a

In the North are ice and snow; b
That is where I'd like to go. b

In the South are birds and flowers; c
There could I have happy hours. c

In the East is the great sea; d
That is where I'd like to be. d

In the West are fields of wheat e
And corn for all of us to eat. e

North, South, East, and West— a
Each has something of the best. a

5. In the poem above, study the line endings to find the rhyme scheme and fill in the blanks provided. Underline the lines of the poem that demonstrate repetition.

Robert Louis Stevenson

I saw you toss the kites on high
And blow the birds about the sky;
And all around I heard you pass,
Like ladies' skirts across the grass—
    O wind, a-blowing all day long,
    O wind, that sings so loud a song!

I saw the different things you did,
But always you yourself you hid.
I felt you push, I heard you call,
I could not see yourself at all—
    O wind, a-blowing all day long,
    O wind, that sings so loud a song!

O you that are so strong and cold,
O blower, are you young or old?
Are you a beast of field and tree,
Or just a stronger child than me?
    O wind, a-blowing all day long,
    O wind, that sings so loud a song!

Think It Through

Give the correct answer.

1. Underline the poetic lines that demonstrate repetition.
2. Fill in the blanks provided to complete the rhyme scheme pattern.

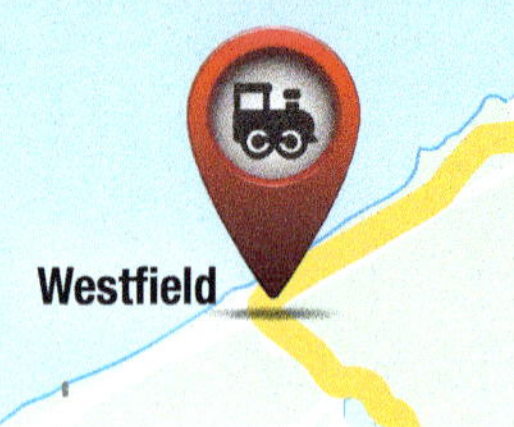

The President's Train Ride

The mid-Atlantic region is rich in U.S. history. Great patriots and dedicated presidents all worked to secure the nation's freedom and independence. One of those remarkable leaders was Abraham Lincoln.

When Abraham Lincoln was nominated[1] to be president, he received an interesting letter from a young supporter from Westfield, New York, who urged Mr. Lincoln to grow a beard so that the ladies would support him. After he was elected, he stopped at Westfield to meet the letter's author, Grace Bedell.

Newspapers published the humorous story on the new president and the young girl that inspired his famous whiskers. Today in Westfield, there is a statue of Lincoln and Bedell to remember their meeting.

[1] nominated—*recommended for election to an office*

NEW YORK WORLD, TUESDAY, FEBRUARY 19, 1861

LINCOLN VISITS NEW YORK

The train bearing the President left Cleveland this morning at 9 o'clock. Quite a large crowd was assembled at the depot and along the line of the track for some distance. The train consisted of one baggage car and three passenger cars, one beautifully carpeted, curtained, and upholstered for the occupancy[2] of the President's party.

At Westfield [a train station in New York] an interesting incident occurred. Shortly after his nomination Mr. Lincoln had received from that place a letter from a little girl, who urged him, as a means of improving his personal appearance, to wear whiskers. Mr. Lincoln at the time replied, stating that although he was obliged by the suggestion, he feared his habits of life were too fixed to admit of even so slight a change as that which letting his beard grow involved. Today, on reaching the place, he related the incident, and said that if that young lady was in the crowd he should be glad to see her. There was a momentary commotion, in the midst of which an old man, struggling through the crowd, approached, leading his daughter, a girl of apparently twelve or thirteen years of age, whom he introduced to Mr. Lincoln as his Westfield correspondent.[3] Mr. Lincoln stooped down and kissed the child, and talked with her for some minutes. Her advice had not been thrown away upon the rugged chieftain.[4] A beard of several months' growth covers (perhaps adorns[5]) the lower part of his face. The young girl's peachy cheek must have been tickled with a stiff whisker, for the growth of which she was herself responsible.

[2] occupancy—*use of a place for a period of time*
[3] correspondent—*one who communicates by writing a letter*
[4] chieftain—*leader*
[5] adorns—*makes more pleasing*

As the train continued traveling, visiting station after station, the reporter recorded the events at each stop. At the last reported depot in Dunkirk, patriotic supporters gathered to show their love for Lincoln and for freedom.

At Dunkirk [station], at the conclusion of a brief speech, Mr. Lincoln, placing his hand upon a flag-staff from which the stars and stripes waved, said, "I stand by the flag of the Union, and all I ask of you is that you stand by me as long as I stand by it." The arches of the depot echoed and re-echoed with the ring of countless cheers. Men swung their hats wildly, women waved their handkerchiefs, and, as the train moved on, the crowd, followed, as if they intended to keep it company to the next station.

Think About It!

Give the correct answer.

1. Where would you find this type of article?
2. Where do the events in this article take place?
3. According to the selection, why did Abraham Lincoln grow a beard for the election?

*4. Did the reporter give his own opinion about the appearance of President Lincoln's beard?

5. How do you know the people at Dunkirk station were supportive of Abraham Lincoln?

What Do YOU Think?

*1. Why do you think President Lincoln was happy to meet Grace Bedell?

*2. How does this news article differ from articles written today?

Grace Bedell's Letter to President Lincoln

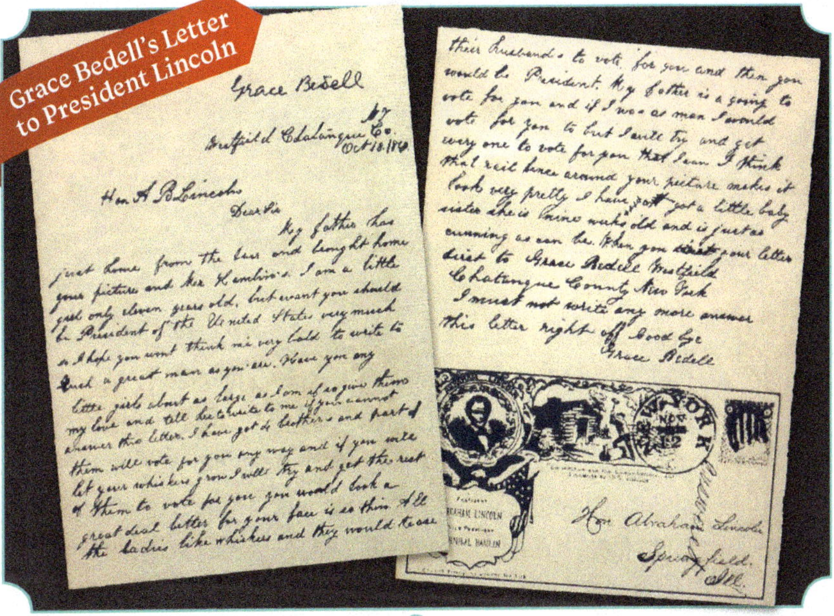

Grace Bedell
Westfield Chatauque Co. NY
Oct 15 1860

Hon A B Lincoln
Dear Sir

My father has just home from the fair and brought home your picture and Mr. Hamlin's. I am a little girl only eleven years old, but want you should be President of the United States very much so I hope you wont think me very bold to write to such a great man as you are. Have you any little girls about as large as I am if so give them my love and tell her to write to me if you cannot answer this letter. I have got 4 brothers and part of them will vote for you any way and if you will let your whiskers grow I will try and get the rest of them to vote for you you would look a great deal better for your face is so thin. All the ladies like whiskers and they would tease their husbands to vote for you and then you would be President. My father is a going to vote for you and if I was a man I would vote for you to but I will try and get every one to vote for you that I can I think that rail fence around your picture makes it look very pretty I have got a little baby sister she is nine weeks old and is just as cunning as can be. When you direct your letter direct to Grace Bedell Westfield Chatauque County New York

I must not write any more answer this letter right off Good bye

Grace Bedell

Hon Abraham Lincoln
Springfield
Ill.

The Jacksons make another historic stop at Dunkirk to tour the Dunkirk Lighthouse and maritime museum. Here they learn about a battle during the War of 1812 in which many British ships were overtaken.

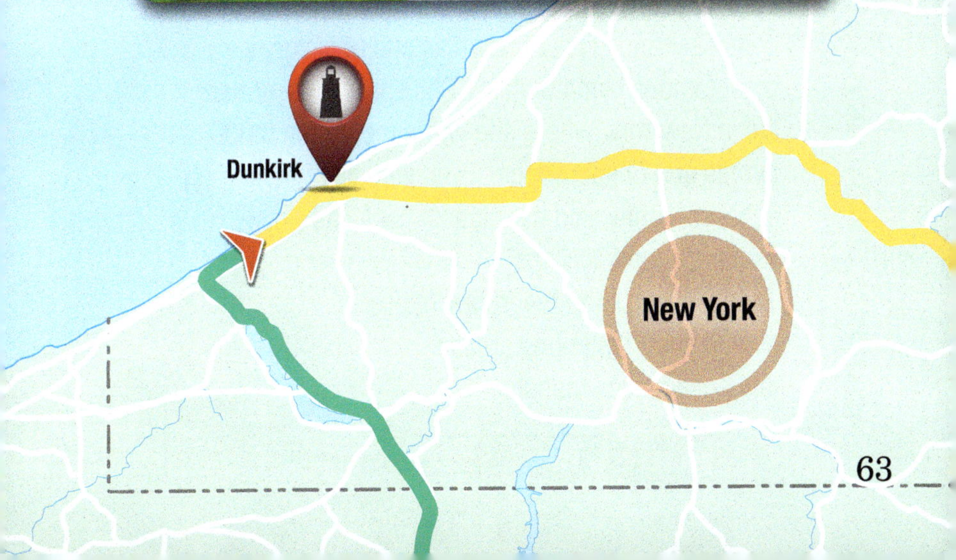

New York

BUILD ON IT

Biography

A biography is a true story about someone's life that was written by another person. Many biographies are written using a sequential text structure and cover many important events throughout the person's entire life. Biographies not only include facts like a birth date and place, but they also could include something the person achieved or how the person influenced others. Like other stories, biographies follow a plot. The details of the plot build up to the climax—sometimes the main character's biggest accomplishment. Finally, the plot will slow down and usually ends with the person's continuing influence in the lives of others.

During the 1800s, a brave and faithful young woman influenced leaders, presidents, and an entire country because of her devotion to Christ and trust in Him. Fanny Crosby was a missionary, poet, and composer and is now known as one of history's most famous hymn writers. She spent most of her life in New York, where she wrote more than 8,000 hymns and Gospel songs. Even with all of her earthly success, Fanny said her biggest goal was winning people to Christ through her hymns. The following short biography retells how Fanny's testimony greatly influenced a new nation.

A Light in the Darkness

Donna M. Covey

A cool stream trickled down a forest pathway. Fanny heard its gurgling sounds, and she giggled with excitement.

"It's cold!" she said as her toes wiggled beneath the sparkling crystal water.

Young Fanny Crosby and her grandmother had taken a morning walk through the meadow and into the woods. Fanny enjoyed these walks, for there were always new things to discover. Today she had found a new plant with heart-shaped leaves. Under the leaves were small flowers whose five soft petals were round on the edges. The plant was growing beside the rock where she was sitting as she dangled her feet in the stream.

"What color are the flowers, Grandma?" Fanny asked.

"Purple," Grandmother replied, "like a distant mountain or the dark sky before a storm, only much brighter. It's called a violet."

"Why is it hiding way back here in the woods?" Fanny inquired.

"It's known as a shy flower," Grandmother recalled, "just content to be its own quiet, lovely self."

"It's kind of like the big old mountains, just sitting there not bothering anything, isn't it, Grandma?"

Grandmother didn't reply. With loving eyes, she watched the little girl who had been her companion these last few years. Tears came to her eyes as she thought about this five-year-old girl with blind eyes who often seemed to "see" more than some people with perfect vision.

"Come along now, Fanny; we must hurry home. You and your mother have to leave bright and early tomorrow morning to catch the ship to the city."

As they began their walk back to the house, Fanny thought about the trip. Because there were no trains in 1825, and the stagecoach did not stop at their little town in New York state, she and her mother were to sail thirty miles down the Hudson River to New York City. There they would go to see an important doctor. Fanny's own doctor had said there might be a chance that Dr. Mott could help her regain her sight. It seemed strange to Fanny to think of seeing things with her own eyes. Her grandmother had been her "eyes" all of her life that she could remember. Grandmother had taught her to recognize the birds by their songs and the trees by their feel and scent. She had described clouds, sunsets, and rainbows so vividly that Fanny was sure she knew just what they looked like.

Fanny had been blind since shortly after her birth. A doctor's mistake was responsible for her blindness, but her family knew that there are no

mistakes in God's plan. They accepted Fanny's blindness and treated her as they would treat any other child. She went hiking, climbed trees, rode horses, and got into mischief just as easily as could any child with sight. Fanny had adjusted so well to her blindness that the idea of seeing things seemed strange to her. Yet, she knew what an exciting experience it would be to view for herself all the wonders her grandmother had described to her. "Maybe someday," she thought, "I'll see that violet for myself!" If not, the trip to the big city would certainly be exciting in itself.

The long ride on a farmer's wagon the next day was hot and bumpy, but when they finally reached the Hudson River, where the ship stood waiting, Fanny's excitement began to increase. She knew immediately that she would enjoy the rest of the trip. She stepped on board, feeling the ship's gentle movement and the cool mist in the air. The trip on the sloop, or small sailing ship, was exciting for Fanny, but not for her mother. Mrs. Crosby became sick shortly after boarding the sloop and had to return to her cabin, where she spent most of the time for the remainder of the trip. Fanny, to her delight, was left in the care of the captain.

The friendliness of the little girl won the captain over at once, and the two spent many enjoyable hours together. The captain was amazed at Fanny's desire to learn. She wanted to know how everything worked and what it was for and how it felt and. . . . He could hardly keep up with her questions. After she had thoroughly explored the ship's controls, Fanny amused the captain by singing songs she had learned. He was amazed that she could remember so many things. She also quoted Scripture passages that she had memorized. Grandmother had often read God's Word to her. Fanny was always desiring to learn more and had made it a point to remember as much as she could. The captain was delighted to listen to her, and in return, he told her sea yarns.[1] The time went by so rapidly that Fanny could hardly believe it when the trip was over.

[1] yarn—*an adventurous tale*

After spending some time with friends in the city, Fanny and her mother went to the doctor's office. The waiting room was a quiet place and strange to her. The smells and even the small noises were unusual to her ears. Medicine always reminded her of sickness and gave her an uneasy feeling in her stomach. She sat quietly playing with the toys that had been put there for young patients, but her mind was busy with other things. What would the doctor do? What would he say? Would she have to stay here? Would she have to go to the hospital? Was it going to hurt?

"Mrs. Crosby, you may come in now," said the strange voice. Fanny took her mother's hand tightly and stood very close to her.

"Well, young lady," said a strong but kind, masculine[2] voice. "Would you like me to make you see?"

All her thoughts in the waiting room came rushing back through her mind. Fear gripped her young heart. "No!" she replied firmly.

"Let's see what we can do," replied the doctor gently, as he noticed the signs of fear on her face. He examined her eyes carefully and thoroughly. As he worked, a grave[3] expression came over him. Then he turned to the mother and spoke.

"Mrs. Crosby, I'm afraid your daughter will never see again."

---

[2]masculine—*manly*
[3]grave—*serious*

After thanking the doctor for his time, Fanny and her mother returned to the ship. When they had finished supper, Fanny went out by the rail and listened to the water splash against their vessel. It would be wonderful to see those waves. Tears started to come to her sightless eyes. But then she thought of all the joys she had already experienced in life. She thought of all the famous people she knew about who had been blind—musicians, poets, and writers. Her mother had told her about them. All these had lived rich, full lives without sight. Just then, a flash of light, just a quick one, came to Fanny's eyes. The sun shining on the waves had a brilliance that penetrated even the darkness of her eyes. It seemed to Fanny that her future could be as bright as the light that glistened on those waves.

In the months and years that followed, life went on much as before. Fanny and her grandmother still enjoyed their walks in the woods, and Grandmother sang hymns with Fanny and taught her more and more of the Bible. Fanny's mother read her the words of the great poets, and before long, Fanny began to shape her own thoughts into verse.[4] When she was eight years old, she wrote her first poem to be published:

> Oh what a happy soul am I!
> Although I cannot see,
> I am resolved that in this world
> Contented I will be.
>
> How many blessings I enjoy
> That other people don't!
> To weep and sigh because I'm blind,
> I cannot, and I won't!

However, one thing about being blind caused her great sorrow. Her friends all went off to school each day, and she was left at home. How she wished that she could learn to read and write! "Dear Lord," she would pray again and again, "please show me how I can learn like other children."

In many ways, Fanny learned much more than other children. By the time she was ten years old, she could recite from memory long passages from the Bible. Sometimes she was able to memorize

[4]verse—*a group of words written as a poem or song*

as many as five chapters a week. She learned to sew and knit, and she continued to learn poetry. However, the desire to go to school never left her.

One afternoon when Fanny was fourteen years old, her mother met her at the gate with surprise in her voice. Fanny could hear a piece of paper rustling in her mother's hands. Had someone written to tell them that a relative had died? No, this was good news. There was a school in New York City called the Institute for the Blind, and Fanny would be able to attend it!

"Oh, thank You, God!" she exclaimed. "He has answered my prayer just as I knew He would!"

Fanny spent many years at the Institute for the Blind, first as a student and then as a teacher. She studied English, history, science, and arithmetic; she learned the works of the great poets; she learned to play the guitar; and she met many important people, including poets, musicians, and presidents. More wonderful to her than any of these things, however, was that while she was at the Institute for the Blind, she found assurance[5] of her salvation in Christ.

Christ brought a brightness into her life much more brilliant than the light she had seen shining on the waves that day in her childhood when she knew that she would never be able to see with her

[5] assurance—*sureness; confidence*

earthly eyes. The joy in her heart overflowed, and she began writing hymns.

During her long life of almost ninety-five years, Fanny Crosby wrote the words to over 8,000 hymns, making her the writer of more published hymns than anyone else in the world. She died in 1915, but Christians all over the world still enjoy singing together such favorites as "Blessed Assurance," "To God Be the Glory," and "Near the Cross." When God opened the spiritual eyes of the blind hymn-writer, He gave to the world a treasure of song that would touch the hearts of multitudes.

John 8:12

"Then spake Jesus again unto them, saying, I am the light of the world: he that followeth Me shall not walk in darkness, but shall have the light of life."

Think About It!

Give the correct answer.

*1. What clues from the text tell you this story is a biography? Explain your answer.

2. Why did Fanny and her mother take a ship to New York City when Fanny was five?

*3. How had Fanny's grandmother "been her 'eyes'"?

4. What did Fanny think was the worst thing about being blind?

5. How was Fanny able to learn like other children?

Character Themes

contentment, gratitude, and faith

Once Fanny Crosby said, "If perfect earthly sight were offered me tomorrow I would not accept it. I might not have sung hymns to the praise of God if I had been distracted by the beautiful and interesting things about me."

She also said, "When I get to Heaven, the first face that shall ever gladden my sight will be that of my Savior."

How would you describe Fanny's attitude?

How did Fanny use her disability for God's glory?

How can faith in God lead to contentment and gratitude?

After reading "A Light in the Darkness," the Jacksons want to take a drive down Foggintown Road in Brewster, New York, to see the historic landmark at the home of Fanny Crosby.

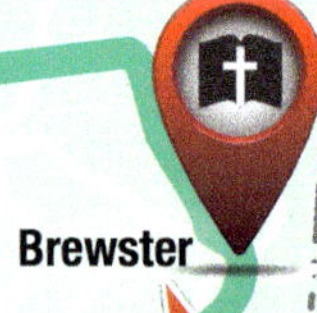

The Best of All

Fanny Crosby

O, the riches vast and boundless
In the Bible we behold!
O, the wealth of joy eternal
Purer than the purest gold;
Just and holy are its counsels;
Truth adorns its every page;
'Tis the lamp that lights our footsteps
In the path from youth to age.

Blessed Bible, sacred treasure,
Precious Book, of all the best;
There is comfort never failing
And a calm, abiding rest.
Read with reverence, and commit it,
Verse by verse, and day by day;
'Tis the word that God has spoken,
And it cannot pass away.

Think About It!

Give the correct answer.

1. Who authored this poem?

*2. What does this poem tell you about the poet?

Near the Cross

Fanny Crosby

Jesus, keep me near the cross,
There a precious fountain;
Free to all, a healing stream
Flows from Calv'ry's mountain.

In the cross, in the cross
Be my glory ever,
Till my raptur'd soul shall find
Rest beyond the river.

Near the cross, a trembling soul,
Love and mercy found me;
There the bright and Morning Star
Sheds His beams around me.

Near the cross, I'll watch and wait,
Hoping, trusting ever,
Till I reach the golden strand
Just beyond the river.

What Do YOU Think?

* Why would Fanny Crosby ask Jesus to keep her "near the cross"?

Never Forget

Savannah Patrick

On September 11, 2001, terrorists[1] attacked the World Trade Center in New York City. Two airplanes flew into the Twin Towers, causing the towers to collapse while thousands of people were inside. Nearly 3,000 people lost their lives during the attack. Today this attack is remembered as the worst terrorist attack in U.S. history. "Never Forget" is a fictional story based on the events that happened on that memorable day.

I stand at the World Trade Center Memorial and remember. It is the anniversary of the terrorist attacks on September 11, 2001. I was only a nine-year-old boy then. Much time has passed, yet it seems like only yesterday that two skyscrapers stood here instead of this memorial. The memorial is lovely—a terraced,[2] manmade waterfall flowing

[1] terrorist—*one who uses violence against others*
[2] terraced—*level areas that look like steps*

deeper and deeper into the ground. Its calming sound echoes out of the chasm[3] into which the water falls. Listening to the water, I can almost forget the horrific sounds from that terrible day. The people around me are silent and thoughtful—much different from how they were the day it all happened.

I was in fourth grade. We had just finished arithmetic for the day and were about to start language when we felt the whole building tremble as if an earthquake were happening. Mr. Hinton's pencil cup jolted from the desk, scattering writing utensils all over the floor. I looked at my friend

[3] chasm—*a deep hole in the ground*

Jaden with a puzzled expression on my face, but he only shrugged. Then, the intercom sounded in our classroom:

"Teachers, we are evacuating the building. Please lead your students downstairs in an orderly fashion."

Some of the girls in my class were crying. I found my friend Jaden, and we filed quickly out of the school behind Mr. Hinton, who could not mask the worry in his eyes. As we exited the building, we saw things that will never be erased from our memories: people crying and pointing, smoke pouring from the top of the World Trade Center's North Tower, a gaping hole in the side of the building. Everyone was confused. What was happening? Jaden and I didn't know what to do, and neither did the adults. We simply stood there in shock beside each other, watching the rescue vehicles scream down the street.

"What's going on? Was it a bomb?" I heard people asking.

Then I saw it. An airplane in the distance—flying strangely low, I thought—coming ever closer to the South Tower.

Suddenly I realized what was happening and shouted, "Look! Look at the plane! It's about to. . . ." But before I could even finish my sentence, the plane flew directly into the South Tower. Another explosion. More trembling. The adults began to realize that these explosions were no accident. New York City was under attack.

Worried parents began arriving, car after car, to take their children home. I heard my name.

"Matt! Matthew Jenkins! Has anyone seen Matthew Jenkins?" It was my eighth-grade brother, Chris.

"Chris!" I called to him wildly. We found each other instantly. I could tell he was shaken as he took my hand and pulled me through the growing crowd. Frantic people from businesses, homes, and schools swarmed the streets, trying to find out what was happening. "Mom is over here," Chris said. "She can't get Dad to answer his phone."

I raced over to my mom. She grabbed me and kissed me all over my head as if I had been lost or something. As she began driving away from the chaos, Chris tried to call my dad on the cellphone over and over again, but there was no answer.

Before long, the traffic was so backed up that we left the car and began jogging, along with hundreds of other people, toward the Brooklyn Bridge. A thundering sound from behind us caused us to stop and turn. All we could see was a dark cloud of debris and smoke billowing our way with tornado-like force. The cloud was so massive it blocked the sun for several minutes. We covered our noses and mouths with our shirts to keep the dust from entering our lungs. When the cloud of dust cleared, we looked toward the World Trade Center. The South Tower was gone—collapsed—reduced to a mountain of rubble.

People shouted and cried in fear around us. Police officers yelled to us to run away and get out of the city. We ran and ran for what seemed like an eternity. Then, just as we thought things couldn't get any worse, the North Tower fell, just like the South Tower. There was another cloud of smoke and another wave of cries and shouting. Now we were all running, fleeing the city, and fearing that more planes would come. I wondered how many lives were already lost. Mom frantically dialed Dad's cellphone number again and again, waiting with failing hope for him to answer. The train he rode to work passed right beneath the World Trade Center—the buildings that had just collapsed. Was Dad underneath all that rubble, or did he survive this horrible attack?

When Dad finally returned Mom's calls, we cried in relief. "Hello? Sharon? Honey, I'm just fine." My mom's eyes gushed with tears of joy. Dad said we would meet on the other side of the bridge.

When we finally found Dad, we were all covered in a thick layer of soot and dust, but none of us were hurt. Dad hugged my brother Chris, kissed my mom, and squeezed as we all held each other tightly.

With tears in her eyes, Mom asked, “Why didn't you answer your phone?”

“I forgot my cellphone this morning and had to run back home. Because of that, I missed my train!”

My mom looked to Heaven and closed her eyes. “Thank You, Lord. Thank You for keeping him safe. Thank You for allowing him to miss his train.”

So, I stand here today at the memorial and remember. The water floods into the footprints of those towers. The sound drowns out the bustle of the city. It reminds me of the day God protected my family and brought an entire nation together in prayer. I will never forget His goodness. I will never forget September 11, 2001.

Think About It!

Give the correct answer.

1. From whose point of view is this story written?
2. Who is the narrator?
3. What is happening at the beginning of the story?

*4. Based on facts given in the story and on what you already know, you can infer how old the narrator would be today. Calculate your answer here.

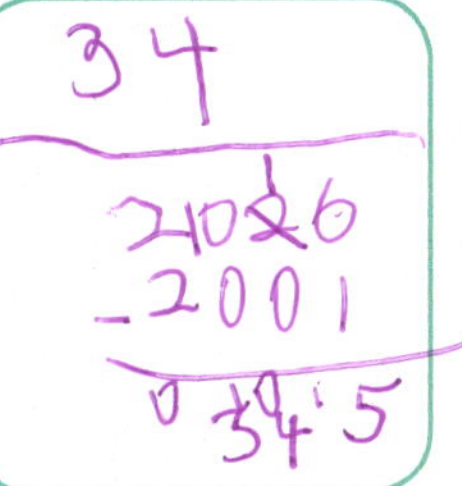

5. What is the story mainly about?

What Do YOU Think?

*1. Why do you think the story is titled "Never Forget"?

*2. Why is it important for people today to remember this event?

John 16:33

"These things I have spoken unto you, that in Me ye might have peace. In the world ye shall have tribulation: but be of good cheer; I have overcome the world."

John 14:27

"Peace I leave with you, My peace I give unto you: not as the world giveth, give I unto you. Let not your heart be troubled, neither let it be afraid."

Every year on the anniversary of the September 11 attacks, two beams of light illuminate the night sky where the towers once stood.

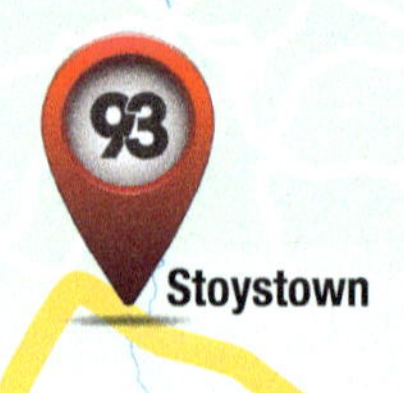

The Tower of Voices

Kayla Sanders

When people tell the story of September 11, 2001, they talk about the World Trade Center and the attacks on the Pentagon in Washington, D.C. However, another tragedy followed a fourth airplane—Flight 93.

Terrorists had taken control of Flight 93, but they did not reach their destination. The forty passengers on the plane fought these men, and the plane crashed in an empty field near Stoystown, Pennsylvania. After many years, the Flight 93 memorial was completed at the site of the crash. In 2018, the Tower of Voices was added to the memorial in honor of the Flight 93 heroes.

The Tower of Voices is ninety-three feet tall and holds forty wind chimes, each with its own unique sound. Think of wind chimes hanging on a porch. Imagine the wind catching the metal rods, causing the chimes to strike. The shorter chimes ring at a high pitch while the longer chimes moan at a low pitch. Their sounds blend into a gentle hum before disappearing altogether. It's a pretty sound, isn't it?

When the wind blows through this mighty tower, the chimes send out sound for miles, reminding all who hear them of the Flight 93 heroes.

Think About It!

Give the correct answer.

1. What clues tell you this selection is informative and written using a descriptive text structure?
2. Where is the Tower of Voices located?
3. How many chimes does the tower hold?
4. What does the Tower of Voices memorialize?

The Old Flag

H. C. Bunner

Off with your hat as the flag goes by!
And let the heart have its say;
You're man enough for a tear in your eye
That you will not wipe away.

You're man enough for a thrill that goes
To your very finger tips;
Ay! the lump just then in your throat that rose
Spoke more than your parted lips.

Lift up the boy on your shoulder high,
And show him the faded shred;
Those stripes are as red as the sunset sky
For the sacrifice of the dead.

Off with your hat as the flag goes by!
Uncover the youngster's head;
Teach him to honor and hold it high
For the sake of the valiant[†] dead.

[†] valiant—*brave*

Theme

honor, respect

John 15:13 "Greater love hath no man than this, that a man lay down his life for his friends."

According to the poem, how can we honor those who have given their lives for our country?

Think About It!

Give the correct answer.

*1. What is the main idea of the poem?

2. Underline the lines of the poem that demonstrate repetition.

3. Fill in the blanks provided to complete the rhyme scheme pattern.

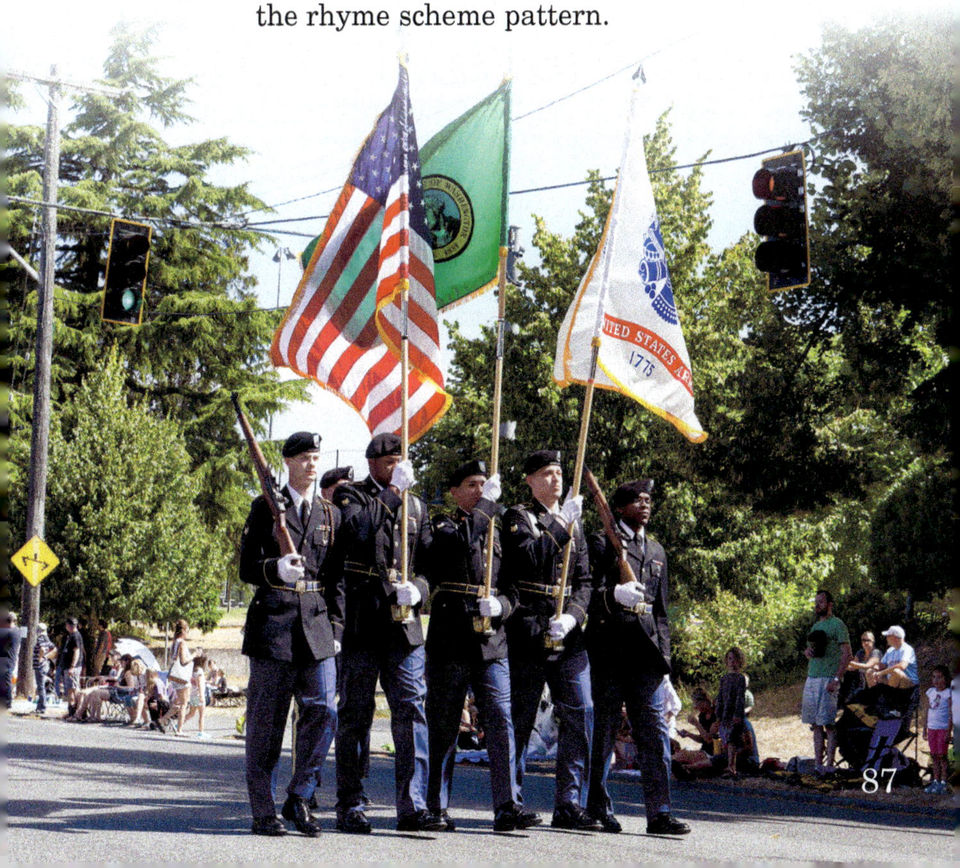

While in Pennsylvania, the Jacksons will stop to visit Independence Hall and the Liberty Bell—the setting for our next story.

Ringing in the Fourth of July

Carolyn Sherwin Bailey

On July 4, 1776, the Declaration of Independence was adopted, declaring the original Thirteen Colonies free from Great Britain. This historical fiction story allows us to see the beginning of our great country through the eyes of a young boy.

The bell ringer of the statehouse in Philadelphia was growing old, and once in a while, his grandson climbed the stairs to the belfry[1] and pulled the bell rope to help him. It was a long, dark way up the dusty staircase, and the lad always went as quietly as his copper-toed shoes would let him, partly so as not to surprise the mice and bats into coming down to meet him and partly to avoid disturbing the

[1] belfry—*a tower or steeple that holds bells*

great men of the country who met in the assembly room of the statehouse.

They were the important statesmen of the American colonies—old Dr. Benjamin Franklin, who could accomplish almost anything from printing an almanac[2] to catching lightning, and Mr. Thomas Jefferson, who was admired as the wise scribe[3] of the colonies. His desk in the statehouse was so covered with quill[4] pens and papers and red seals that the lad scarcely dared to dust it. There was also Mr. John Adams of Massachusetts, who had seen a shipload of bales of tea turned overboard in Boston Harbor three years before because the colonists refused to pay a tax on it to King George III of England. John Adams loved a cup of fragrant tea served in Boston's blue and white china, but he loved his country more.

---

[2]almanac—*a yearly calendar containing useful information*
[3]scribe—*a writer; author*
[4]quill—*the hollow stem of a feather*

On his way up toward the belfry stairs, the bell ringer's grandson peered in the door at these men and others with them in knee breeches,[5] silver-buckled shoes, and powdered hair. They were the members of the Second Continental Congress, and their talk was of the colonies they represented—what was best for them in the way of government that the people might be free and yet united. The idea had already come to this first body of lawmakers that laws should not be made to limit a man's freedom but to give men new liberty to live and work and think by freeing them from wrong-doing, lawlessness, and crime.

This matter of governing a new nation was becoming increasingly important. The Congress realized that, and so the members of Congress met in the statehouse of old Philadelphia on a very warm summer afternoon, the fourth of July in the year 1776.

The lad turned away from the door. Perhaps it would be better not to ring the bell for sunset, because the Congress was sitting so late, he decided. His grandfather was up in the belfry polishing the bell, and he would wait and go up when the gentlemen of the Congress started home. The boy stood a little while in the doorway of the brick building and looked down Chestnut Street on which it stood.

[5] breeches—*knee-length pants*

There came the post rider, his mail pouches gray with dust and his horse's hooves striking sparks on the paving stones in the warm, gathering twilight. What an adventuresome life a post rider's was, the lad thought enviously. They rode between all the cities of the colonies, meeting at the borders to exchange and carry on letters and packets.

The post riders were making and living the geography of the American colonies, which were too young and growing up too fast to be between book covers or on maps yet in the schools. They rode to the green pasture land of New Hampshire, heard the whir of spinning wheels in Connecticut, and passed the gate of Harvard College in Boston. They talked to the fishermen of Rhode Island and the trappers of New York, stopped for foaming mugs of milk in some dairy of New Jersey or Pennsylvania. They passed fertile farms of Delaware and Maryland, had suppers of hot cornbread and ham on a rich Virginia plantation, and rode past white cotton fields in the Carolinas or Georgia. The thirteen thriving, growing, alert American colonies were alike in their desire for liberty and different in their settlement, people, work, products, and mode of thinking. But they were keeping together after a fashion, for they all sent delegates[6] to the Second Continental Congress here in Philadelphia, and they were

[6] delegate—*a person sent to represent others at a meeting*

united at heart in a league of neighborly friendship and for common defense.

The post rider was gone now. The lad in the door of the statehouse could see nothing but a cloud of gray dust up Chestnut Street where he had been. It was the quiet, dim end of a sultry[7] day, and the street was empty, for the early supper tables would soon be laid. At least Chestnut Street had been empty. Now the boy saw that it was suddenly beginning to fill. Housewives who had neglected to take off their cooking aprons, shopkeepers with their tape measures still dangling over their shoulders, a raw recruit[8] of a soldier who held his musket awkwardly because his hands were more used to a spade, a barrister[9] in a long black robe and huge wig, even the post rider returned—all these and more moved toward the stately old building that housed the Congress. "What could it mean?" the bell ringer's grandson wondered, shrinking back into the shadow of the doorway.

As he waited, the door of the assembly room opened, and he saw that Mr. Thomas Jefferson held in his hand a very long and important-looking document from which he was reading in his strong, clear voice. The boy could catch some of the words and so could that part of the crowd outside nearest the open windows.

---

[7] sultry—*hot and moist*
[8] raw recruit—*inexperienced, newly enlisted soldier*
[9] barrister—*a lawyer*

Mr. Jefferson read:

"When, in the course of human events, it becomes necessary for one people to dissolve the political bands which have connected them with another, and to assume, among the powers of the earth, the separate and equal station to which the laws of nature and of nature's God entitle them.

"We, therefore, the representatives of the United States of America in general Congress assembled, appealing to the Supreme Judge of the world for the rectitude[10] of our intentions, do, in the name, and by authority of the good people of these colonies, solemnly publish and declare, that these United colonies are, and of right ought to be free and independent states."

That was the word that held the crowd breathless: "independent."

[10] rectitude—*strict honesty; correctness*

Then Mr. Jefferson finished:—

"That as free and independent States, they have full power to levy[11] war, conclude peace, contract alliances,[12] establish commerce,[13] and to do all other acts and things which independent States may do. And, for the support of this declaration, with a firm reliance[14] on the protection of Divine Providence,[15] we mutually pledge to each other our lives, our fortunes, and our sacred honor."

There was a silence of only a second. Then the ayes[16] of the Congress, pledging the new nation's support to this Declaration of Independence filled the room, resounded in the street, and echoed from the crowd, mingling with their cheers.

"Ring the bell for freedom!" someone shouted.

The bell ringer's grandson ran up the stairs to the belfry, kicking up almost as much dust as the post rider and not one whit[17] afraid of the scurrying mice and the flapping winged bats.

"Ring the bell, Grandfather," he cried. "The Congress and the people say, Ring it for freedom!"

Taking hold of the rope, the lad pulled too, helping his grandfather with all his might as peal[18]

---

[11] levy—*engage in*

[12] alliance—*a promise between two or more countries to fight together against their enemies in time of war*

[13] commerce—*buying and selling*

[14] reliance—*dependence*

[15] Divine Providence—*God's guidance and control*

[16] aye—*"yes" vote*

[17] whit—*smallest bit*

[18] peal—*the sound of the ringing of a set of bells*

after peal rang out through the summer evening as a signal for more shouts of joy in the street and the pealing of every other bell in old Philadelphia.

There are Christmas bells that chime for peace and church bells that call us to think of holy things. The sheep bells tinkling along country lanes at sunset tell us of the plenty and comfort of the farm. But the ringing of the Liberty Bell on that first Fourth of July held the message of all these others. It sounded the desire for a day when wars would not be needed. It rang for religious and civil liberty, for the right to enjoy play and work without autocratic[19] interference, and for freedom to develop

[19]autocratic—*government*

and enjoy all the prosperity[20] that the fertile earth offered. So it rings today and will always ring in the hearts of free peoples.

It was a very fine way of celebrating a great day, particularly for the lad who was able to have a part in it. No one thought about wasting money on fire-crackers or popguns or rockets, for the people of the colonies saw a long road ahead of them before they should be able to work out their independence. The call of the Liberty Bell was all the celebration they wanted or needed to start them along that road. The next year, though, saw them holding the flag that Congress had adopted. Thirteen broad red and white stripes and thirteen white stars, circled in a blue field stood for the thirteen original American colonies and waved for freedom.

[20]prosperity—*success*

Theme

patriotism

The men of the Second Continental Congress adopted an important declaration out of love for their country.

How can you, like the Founding Fathers, show your patriotism?

Think About It!

Give the correct answer.

1. Who met in the statehouse to discuss the governing of the new nation?
2. Name some of the men in this assembly.
3. In what city did this meeting take place?
4. Who wrote the Declaration of Independence?
5. What did the boy and his grandfather do after they heard the Declaration?
6. What was the bell called? Why was that a good name for the bell?

What Do YOU Think?

*1. In the Declaration of Independence, the Founding Fathers mentioned the "Supreme Judge of the world" and "Divine Providence." Why was it important to include these names in the Declaration of Independence?

*2. What happens when God is left out of judgments and decisions that are made?

Psalm 121:2

"My help cometh from the LORD,
Which made heaven and earth."

God Bless Our Native Land

Charles T. Brooks and John S. Dwight

God bless our native land! *a*
Firm may she ever stand, *a*
Through storm and night: *b*
When the wild tempests rave, *c*
Ruler of wind and wave, *c*
Do Thou our country save *c*
By Thy great might! *b*

For her our prayers shall rise *d*
To God, above the skies;
On Him we wait:
Thou Who art ever nigh
Guarding with watchful eye,
To Thee aloud we cry,
"God save the State!"

Theme

dependence on God

The Second Continental Congress declared their dependence on God, and many American patriots since then have done the same. You will recognize this theme in the poem "God Bless Our Native Land."

Which lines in the poem show a dependence on God?

Think It Through

Give the correct answer.

In the blanks provided, write the rhyme scheme.

Daniel and the Lions' Den

Daniel 6

The strength of great leaders comes from a dependence on God. For their family Bible time, the Jacksons will read from the book of Daniel. Daniel is a written testimony of how God can work even in a sinful nation when one man honors Him. As you read chapter six of Daniel, look for other leaders and the influence that they have on their king and nation.

It pleased Darius to set over the kingdom an hundred and twenty princes, which should be over the whole kingdom; and over these three presidents; of whom Daniel was first: that the princes might give accounts unto them, and the king should have no damage.

Then this Daniel was preferred above the presidents and princes, because an excellent spirit was in him; and the king thought to set him over the whole realm.[1]

Then the presidents and princes sought to find occasion[2] against Daniel concerning the kingdom; but they could find none occasion nor fault; forasmuch as he was faithful, neither was there any error or fault found in him. Then said these men, We shall not find any occasion against this Daniel, except we find it against him concerning the law of his God.

Then these presidents and princes assembled together to the king, and said thus unto him, King Darius, live for ever.

All the presidents of the kingdom, the governors, and the princes, the counsellors, and the captains, have consulted together to establish a royal statute,[3] and to make a firm decree, that whosoever shall ask a petition[4] of any God or man for thirty days, save of thee, O king, he shall be cast into the den of lions.

Now, O king, establish the decree, and sign the writing, that it be not changed, according to the law of the Medes and Persians, which altereth[5] not.

Wherefore king Darius signed the writing and the decree.

[1] realm—*kingdom*
[2] occasion—*a cause or reason*
[3] statute—*law*
[4] petition—*request*
[5] altereth—*changes*

Now when Daniel knew that the writing was signed, he went into his house; and his windows being open in his chamber toward Jerusalem, he kneeled upon his knees three times a day, and prayed, and gave thanks before his God, as he did aforetime.[6]

Then these men assembled, and found Daniel praying and making supplication[7] before his God.

Then they came near, and spake before the king concerning the king's decree; Hast thou not signed a decree, that every man that shall ask a petition of any God or man within thirty days, save of thee, O king, shall be cast into the den of lions? The king answered and said, The thing is true, according to the law of the Medes and Persians, which altereth not.

[6] aforetime—*previously*
[7] supplication—*a humble request*

Then answered they and said before the king, That Daniel, which is of the children of the captivity of Judah, regardeth not thee, O king, nor the decree that thou hast signed, but maketh his petition three times a day.

Then the king, when he heard these words, was sore displeased with himself, and set his heart on Daniel to deliver him: and he labored till the going down of the sun to deliver him.

Then these men assembled unto the king, and said unto the king, Know, O king, that the law of the Medes and Persians is, That no decree nor statute which the king establisheth may be changed.

Then the king commanded, and they brought Daniel, and cast him into the den of lions. Now the king spake and said unto Daniel, Thy God whom thou servest continually, He will deliver thee.

And a stone was brought, and laid upon the mouth of the den; and the king sealed it with his own signet, and with the signet of his lords; that the purpose might not be changed concerning Daniel.

Then the king went to his palace, and passed the night fasting:[8] neither were instruments of music brought before him: and his sleep went from him.

Then the king arose very early in the morning, and went in haste unto the den of lions.

And when he came to the den, he cried with a lamentable[9] voice unto Daniel: and the king spake

[8]fasting—*eating very little or no food while spending time in prayer*
[9]lamentable—*very regretful*

and said to Daniel, O Daniel, servant of the living God, is thy God, whom thou servest continually, able to deliver thee from the lions?

Then said Daniel unto the king, O king, live for ever.

My God hath sent his angel, and hath shut the lions' mouths, that they have not hurt me: forasmuch as before him innocency was found in me; and also before thee, O king, have I done no hurt.

Then was the king exceeding glad for him, and commanded that they should take Daniel up out of the den. So Daniel was taken up out of the den, and no manner of hurt was found upon him, because he believed in his God.

. . . Then king Darius wrote unto all people, nations, and languages, that dwell in all the earth;

Peace be multiplied unto you.
I make a decree, That in every dominion of my kingdom men tremble and fear before the God of Daniel: for He is the living God, and stedfast for ever, and His kingdom that which shall not be destroyed, and His dominion shall be even unto the end. He delivereth and rescueth, and He worketh signs and wonders in Heaven and in earth, who hath delivered Daniel from the power of the lions.

So this Daniel prospered in the reign of Darius, and in the reign of Cyrus the Persian.

Think About It!

Give the correct answer.

1. Why did King Darius trust Daniel to be ruler over the whole realm?
2. What did the presidents and princes ask the king to decree?
3. What were the presidents' and princes' intentions when asking the king to issue the decree?
4. When the king found out Daniel was not following orders, ____.
   a. he signed a new statute
   b. he threw Daniel out of the kingdom
   c. he was upset with himself
   d. the Bible doesn't say
5. What was the end result of Daniel's choice to obey God?

*6. Why do you think God recorded this story in His Word?

Washington, D.C.

In the heart of Washington, D.C., you will find a museum overflowing with biblical history. At the entrance to the Museum of the Bible are the Gutenberg Gates displaying the first eighty lines of the book of Genesis written in Latin.

To BUILD ON IT, see page 195.

A Home-Cooked Meal

Bethany Urbina

Before long, the little van was rolling over the southern country roads. It passed several wide fields lined with budding crops before it turned onto a long driveway. Caleb and Christy could see a red brick home at the end of the driveway with rocking chairs on the porch.

"Are we stopping here?" asked Christy.

"Yes, we are! This is Uncle Bill's house," answered Mom.

"I don't remember an Uncle Bill," said Caleb in confusion.

"Oh, he's not really an uncle!" Mom explained. "Bill and his wife, Lacey, were great friends of your grandparents, my mother and father. Growing up, I always called him Uncle Bill."

"Uncle Bill has grandchildren about your age!" added Dad. "I think you will get to meet them today."

Caleb and Christy shared an excited look in the back seat. It had been many days since they had talked to anyone their own age. Before the van stopped at the end of the driveway, a friendly, gray-haired man stepped out onto the porch and waved. The Jackson family climbed out of the van and hurried to meet him. A small, white-haired woman with glasses appeared on the porch. She squealed and ran to Mom, hugging her tightly and dabbing under her glasses with a handkerchief.

"My, my! Look at you, Sarah!" Aunt Lacey said fondly. "All grown-up with your own family!"

"Who are these good-looking people with you, Sarah?" teased Uncle Bill while adding a hug of his own.

"Well, you remember my husband. . . . And these are my children, Christy, Caleb, and little Cole," Mom answered, pointing to everyone.

"Y'all are just in time for the cookout!" said Uncle Bill to Caleb and Christy. "Come on back! I hope you're hungry!"

The Jackson family followed Uncle Bill and Aunt Lacey into the backyard where the smell of hot dogs cooking on the grill made their stomachs growl. Uncle Bill introduced his grandson, David, to Caleb. David was from North Carolina and told Caleb stories of deep sea fishing and seeing humpback whales off the coast. Christy helped Aunt Lacey and her granddaughter, Ruby, bring out plates, silverware, and a pitcher of sweet tea to the picnic table. When the food was ready and everyone was seated, Uncle Bill stood up and gave thanks to God for His many blessings. After he was finished, Caleb couldn't help but notice Mom's face. He couldn't tell if Mom was happy or sad.

"What is it, Mom?" Caleb asked quietly. Mom smiled at Caleb and gave his hand a gentle squeeze.

"I think that, so far," she answered with a sniff, "this is my favorite stop."

Think About It!

Give the correct answer.

1. Who was Uncle Bill?
2. Where were Uncle Bill's grandchildren from?
3. Why do you think this was Mrs. Jackson's favorite stop?

Southeast

Let's travel down old country roads, visit the frontier, and explore the southern mountains as the Jacksons visit the southeastern region of the United States. There will be breathtaking views, biblical encounters, and even some adventure from the Carolina and Tennessee frontiers.

Smoky Mountains

Humpback Whale

Country Road

Deep Sea Fishing

Virginia

While the Jacksons are in Williamsburg, Virginia, they will stop at the Back Forty Bees Honey Farm where they will learn how beehives are kept and how honey is made.

Williamsburg

Compare and Contrast Text Structure

Remember that an author has a purpose for writing before he starts to write. When an author wants to write an **informative selection** and compare two items or ideas, he uses a compare and contrast text structure. This means the author will write about the ways two items are the same or similar by **comparing** them and the ways they are different by **contrasting** them. Signal words that are often used to compare and contrast include *both*, *similar*, *different*, *like*, *unlike*, and *while*.

Example:

Jogging and swimming are both great ways to exercise. They both strengthen your muscles, but swimming can be easier on the joints than jogging. While you are swimming, your body makes little contact with hard surfaces, but while you are jogging, your feet are always hitting a hard floor or pavement. However, jogging can usually be done more often than swimming. Unlike swimming, you can jog anywhere, even in place. A pool isn't always nearby for swimming.

The example gives the reader important information he needs to know about the two topics, jogging and swimming. This paragraph was written to help the reader make an informed decision based on the information he was given—whether to exercise by jogging or swimming. Many other compare and contrast selections are written for the same reason.

Think It Through

Give the correct answer.

1. Which idea refers to looking at the way two items are different?

   a. comparing   b. contrasting

2. How does jogging *compare* to swimming?

3. If you were to *contrast* the two activities, what would you say about them?

4. On page 113, pick two of your favorite school subjects and write one in each circle. **Compare** and **contrast** the two subjects.

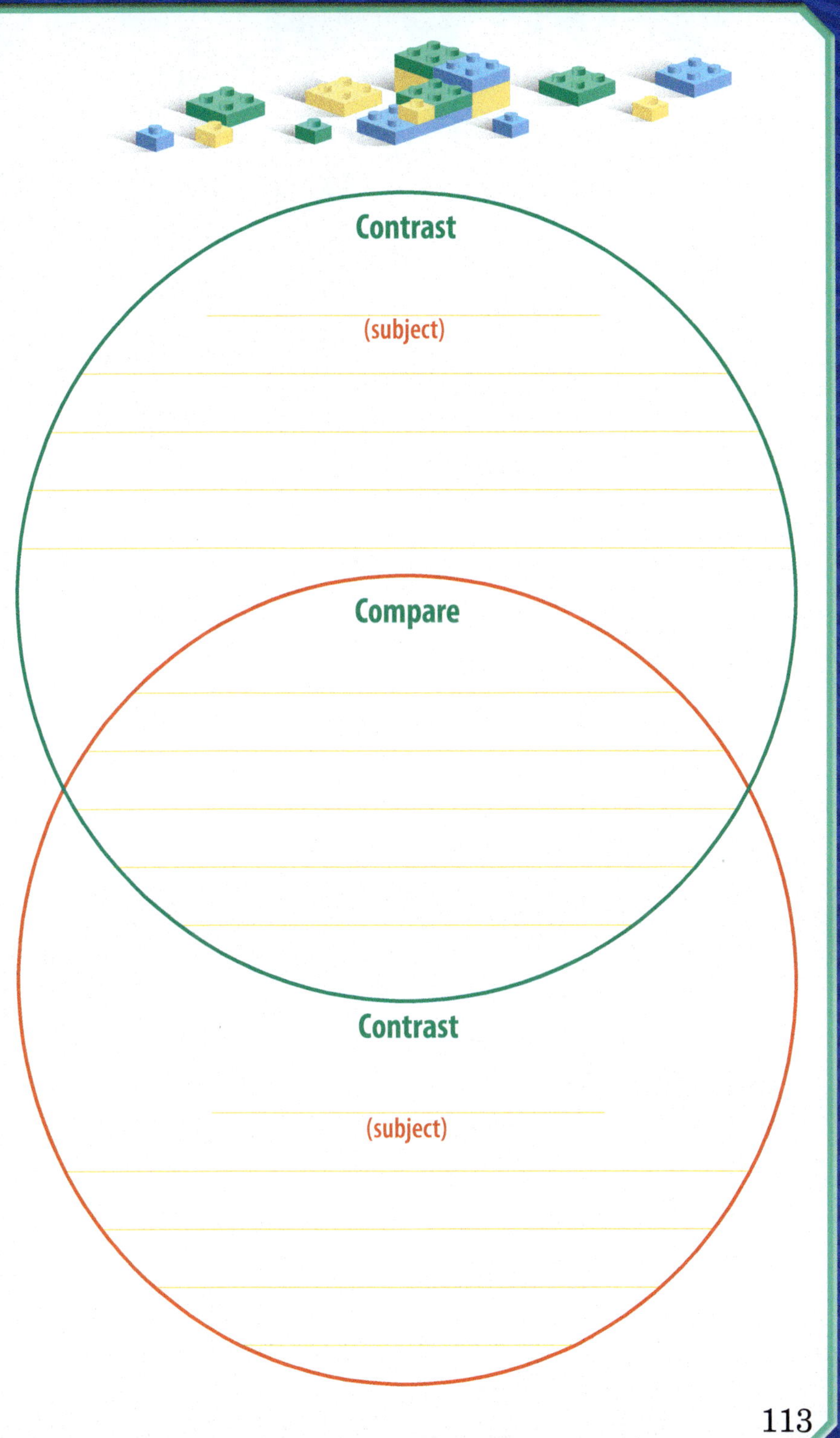
Contrast
(subject)
Compare
Contrast
(subject)

Sweet Treats

Kayla Sanders

Which would you choose—cake or pie? Slush or milkshake? Cookie or brownie? Maple syrup or honey? You probably didn't have to think twice to know which of these you preferred. Most of these sweet treats have to be mixed, prepared, and some even baked before you can enjoy them, but two of them can be found in abundance in nature.

Maple syrup and honey *both* come from natural sources. Maple syrup is made from a sweet water-like liquid found in maple trees. People collect this clear liquid by connecting a piping system across hundreds of acres of maple trees. Once the liquid drips from the trees, it is boiled to produce the desired flavor and color of maple syrup. As it is processed, the liquid thickens into syrup.

Unlike maple syrup, honey is handcrafted by honeybees all over the world. The honeybee collects nectar from flowers, and once it has collected enough nectar, it takes the collection back to the hive. At the hive, the collected nectar is processed by bees and stored in the honeycomb where it thickens into honey. You can eat it straight from the honeycomb!

***Both* of these sweet treats are graded by their appearance.** Just like tests can be graded with an *A*, *B*, *or C*, honey and maple syrup get a grade before they are sent to the grocery store. This grade represents the quality, flavor, and even the color of the honey and maple syrup. Generally, lighter colors taste milder, and darker colors taste richer. Experts claim that the best maple syrup is thin and golden in color, *while* honey is best when it looks mostly clear. Cloudy honey is graded at a lower level.

Honey and maple syrup are *both* commonly used today, but their uses *differ*. Maple syrup is commonly drizzled on pancakes, *while* honey is often used to sweeten a homemade buttermilk biscuit or a skillet full of fresh cornbread. *Both* honey and maple syrup can be mixed into ice cream and even into soap!

Now that you know the *similarities* and *differences*, which would you choose—maple syrup or honey?

Although the Bible doesn't speak of maple syrup, it actually makes several references to honey. In the Psalms, David sings that God's Word is sweeter than honey and the honeycomb, and it is his delight. Have you ever thought about that? That's pretty sweet!

Think About It!

Give the correct answer.

1. What type of story is "Sweet Treats?" Circle your answer(s) in the chart below. Explain your answer.

Text Structures	
Narrative	Informative—nonfiction
Fiction	Descriptive
Nonfiction	Sequential
	Compare and Contrast

2. What is the selection about?

To BUILD ON IT, see page 196.

Elizabeth Irvine's Ride

Author Unknown

You have probably heard of the famous ride of Paul Revere from Boston to Lexington in 1775. But you may not have heard of another important ride by a courageous patriot around the same time. This exciting story takes place in a historical setting. The characters and main event are real, but the details, thoughts, and feelings described in the plot are imagined by the author. Enjoy this historical fictional retelling of Elizabeth Irvine's Ride.

Elizabeth Ann was a bright, black-eyed girl who lived in Virginia many years ago when the beautiful Shenandoah[1] Valley was covered with forests instead of smiling farmlands as it is today. She loved to play about under the great trees with her brothers and sisters, and she often longed to ride along the western trail that led over the mountains.

"Someday I shall ride and ride into the blue hills of the sunset," she said. But she knew that dangers lurked in the wild beyond their plantation at Deerfield. At night she could hear the howling of wolves in the woods. She had heard much talk of the native people in the countryside and wondered who of them were friends or foe. From the time she was a very little girl, she had been used to seeing them filing over the trail in their bright blankets

[1] Shenandoah (shĕn′ən·dō′ə)

and moccasins. Sometimes they looked fierce in paint and feathers, and sometimes they spoke kind words as friends.

One day when Elizabeth was a little girl about eight years old, the children were playing merrily in the woods. Suddenly an elderly native woman stepped out from behind a tree and said, "Me Shawnee Kate—much hungry." While the other children hid away in fright, Elizabeth came running back, her little pinafore[2] filled with corn-pone[3] and apples.

After that, Shawnee Kate appeared again and again. Sometimes she would nod to Elizabeth and pass by without speaking. Sometimes she would ask for a drink from the well.

Elizabeth would bring her something to eat and say, "It must be a hungry walk over the hills. Some day I am going along the trail, and maybe then you will give me something by your campfire."

"Kate not forget," said the native woman.

The years passed and Elizabeth did go over the trail—to a home of her own. The day came when she put her hand in Francis Irvine's and went with him to the clearing called Long Glade. She rode away on her horse, Dundee, a present from her father.

---

[2] pinafore—*a sleeveless, apron-like garment*
[3] cornpone—*flat bread made of ground corn*

"I have often longed to ride this way," she said to her young husband; "and now it is truly my trail—the way to my new home."

The days at Long Glade were happy and busy. There was no time to be lonely, not even when she was alone in the cabin from morning till night. She sang as she spun her linen and carded the wool that was to make clothes for herself and her husband. The pewter[4] plates, too, that shone like silver on the dresser, proved her a good housewife.

One day her husband said, "We are all going on a long hunting trip. It is just the time to get our winter's supply of venison.[5] If we don't get our share now, Kill Buck's braves will not leave a deer on the mountain."

For the first time, the new home seemed very lonely. Young Mrs. Irvine found herself thinking all that afternoon, as she wove her wool and linen into stout linsey-woolsey,[6] of the days when she had played with her sisters about the old home at Deerfield.

A shadow fell across the doorway. There was a native woman standing there.

"Why, Kate!" cried Elizabeth in amazement. "I thought you were with your people at South Branch. I didn't know you were in this part of the country. Come in and rest."

---

[4]pewter—*an alloy of tin with lead, brass, or copper*

[5]venison—*deer meat*

[6]linsey-woolsey—*rough cloth made from wool and cotton or linen*

"No rest," said the old woman. "I come to tell you. Kill Buck makes ready to attack Deerfield."

Elizabeth raised her hand toward the great dinner horn. Then she remembered; all the men of the little settlement were away chasing deer on the mountain. She looked out to where the western sun was dropping behind the trees. It was thirty miles to Deerfield; it would be dark before she could go half the way. There was no time for waiting and thinking. There was but one thing to do. She ran to the pasture lot. "Dundee! Dundee! Come, Dundee!" she called. The horse galloped up, whinnying joyfully as she held out the bridle and buckled the saddle firmly on his back. "It's for Deerfield, Dundee!" she called to him softly, bending low over his neck as they started along the trail.

"It's a rough trail," she said to herself, as the horse stumbled in the gathering dusk, "but it's *my* trail, and God will bring us safely through the dark."

Thirty miles is indeed a long way over a rough forest road. Darkness had closed about her before she left the headwaters of the Glade. It was midnight when she came to the first mountain path, Buffalo Gap. Dundee had to feel his way, dodging rocks and stumps. With his wonderful "horse sense" he kept to the trail in spite of the briary[7] undergrowth and overhanging branches that jealously struggled to cover up the man-made way through the wilderness.

Now an owl hooted directly overhead. Again and again came the howls of wolves disturbed by the strange invasion of the dark forest. Elizabeth shivered as she thought that some of Kill Buck's tribe might be hiding there, too.

There were eight more miles to go after the passing at Buffalo Gap. Elizabeth bent over and patted her horse's neck. "Good Dundee," she said, "you'll take me safely, I know."

[7] briary—*full of briars; prickly*

All at once the horse almost stopped, then plunged suddenly forward into a stream of running water.

"Oh, Dundee, we're at Calf Pasture River, and we're almost home!" cried Elizabeth. The road was all well known now, and Dundee cantered[8] on with renewed strength.

At last, just as the morning star appeared over the Blue Ridge, Dundee and his rider came within sight of Deerfield. "Weeping may last for a night, but joy comes in the morning," thought Elizabeth.

She had reached her old home, and the settlement was saved.

---

[8] canter—*to ride at an easy gallop*

Think About It!

Give the correct answer.

1. What was Elizabeth's girlhood dream?
2. With what duties did Elizabeth occupy her day in her new home?
3. Why did Shawnee Kate warn Elizabeth about the attack?
4. Where did Kill Buck plan to attack?
5. How did Elizabeth show bravery and courage?

*6. What parts of this historical fiction are real?
   a. characters
   b. details
   c. events
   d. feelings
   e. thoughts

Elizabeth Irvine as well as many other early patriots had a strong faith in God and His Word. They worshiped in the earliest churches built in our nation. Not far from Deerfield in Jamestown, Virginia, you will find the Memorial church. The tower attached to the front of the church remains from the first church of the early 1700s—Jamestown Church. This is the oldest structure still remaining in Jamestown.

Virginia

Jamestown

North Carolina

Along the way, we might trek through the Blue Ridge Mountains located along the border of Tennessee and North Carolina and enjoy some breathtaking views. Many small towns and villages dot the landscape of this scenic part of America.

Chimney Rock Park

Kayla Sanders

Unexpected discoveries are often made on the backroads and in the smallest towns of the United States. North Carolina is home to Chimney Rock Mountain, a popular tourist destination.

Along the edge of North Carolina's Blue Ridge Mountains, you can visit an unusual rock formation that looks like a chimney. This large rock that juts out from the famous mountain range is 315 feet tall, soaring 2,280 feet above sea level. Five walking trails in Chimney Rock State Park can take you to the top. Some trails, like the Great Woodland Adventure Trail, for instance, with its twelve discovery stations, are easier for families. Some are much harder, like the Outcroppings Trail consisting of almost 500 steps to climb and three different lookout points—the Grotto, the Subway, and Pulpit Rock.

While hiking to the top of Chimney Rock is good exercise, your younger siblings may not be able to climb that far. But don't worry. You can take the elevator! An elevator inside Chimney Rock can take you to the top in less than a minute!

Whether you hike or ride the elevator, the view at the top is breathtaking. You might be able to catch a glimpse of a peregrine falcon as it leaves the nest and soars on wind currents looking for its dinner. You can

see Hickory Nut Falls, a 404-foot-tall waterfall, spilling over the side of Chimney Rock Mountain. Lake Lure, a nearby, manmade lake, can easily be spotted from the top of Chimney Rock. On a clear, sunny day, you may be able to see up to seventy-five miles across the Blue Ridge Mountains and the Piedmont area of North Carolina.

New adventures are around every corner. Keep your eyes wide open as you look for the next discovery on your road trip east!

Think About It!

Give the correct answer.

1. What text structure was used to write this selection? How do you know?
2. Knowing the text structure of this selection reminds me to _____.
   a. enjoy the story
   b. find the moral
   c. look for details
3. Where is this park located?
4. What is the height of Chimney Rock?
   a. 12 feet b. 315 feet c. 2,280 feet
5. Which trail in the park would be the most challenging for hikers?
   a. Great Woodland Adventure Trail
   b. Outcroppings Trail
   c. Subway
6. What park feature allows younger children to see the top of Chimney Rock?

The tallest natural sand dune system in the Eastern United States is Jockey's Ridge located in Nags Head, North Carolina. Tourists love to play on and around these dunes, some of them 80 to 100 feet tall!

North Carolina

Nags Head

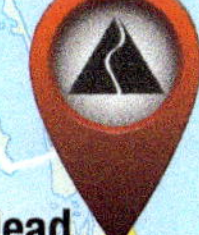

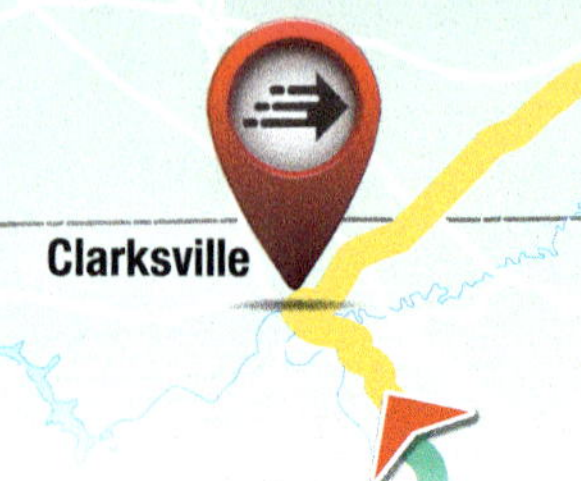

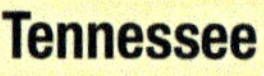

Wilma Rudolph

Cheryl Reid

In the small southern town of Clarksville, Tennessee, we find this heartwarming true story of a young girl who faced incredible obstacles and was determined to overcome them.

Wilma lay on the hospital table as Nurse Mary massaged her leg, stretching and working the weak muscles that kept Wilma from walking on her own without a brace. Two times a week, Wilma Rudolph and her mother traveled fifty miles by bus from their home in Clarksville, Tennessee, to a hospital in Nashville for therapy.

Wilma's leg muscles had been paralyzed from a disease called polio. Polio affected people differently depending on the part of the body that the disease weakened. While Wilma's leg muscles were affected, others suffering from polio might not be able to use their arms or might have trouble breathing.

Each morning when Wilma woke, the first thing she did was put on her brace that allowed her to walk. While her brothers and sisters did chores or played outside, Wilma watched. She tried to be cheerful and encouraging to her family, but what she really wanted to do was play outside like the other children. Because she was determined to walk without her brace, she made herself take each step without limping and tried not to think about the pain. Wilma didn't realize it, but with every painful step, she was strengthening her leg muscles.

Since Wilma's illness had made her body weak, she was unable to start school until she was seven years old. On her first day of school, Wilma nervously entered the second-grade classroom hoping that someone would look beyond her brace and want to be her friend. When a girl named Nancy Bower took Wilma's hand and asked her to play a game, Wilma knew that she would be all right.

The trips to Nashville went from two times a week down to one. Finally, one Sunday morning before church, Wilma took off her brace and put it away. She had never been more nervous or more excited. She would walk into the church building on her own without any help. She worried as she got dressed and brushed her hair, hoping she wouldn't trip and fall in front of everyone.

When Wilma arrived at church, she took a deep breath, walked through the door and down the aisle, and took her seat with her family while the entire church congregation clapped and cheered.

Wilma's trips to the Nashville hospital continued, but so did her treatments at home. As Wilma's muscles became stronger, she wanted to play basketball with her friends. When she entered the seventh grade, Wilma made her high school basketball team, although she did not play in any games until she was older. Coach Gray, her basketball coach, decided to start a girls' track team. Wilma joined because she thought running would be fun. What she didn't expect is that she would be so good at it!

Although Wilma continued playing basketball and even helped her team win the state championship, she found that running track was her best sport. When a college track coach watched Wilma run, he knew that she had a special gift. Coach Temple invited Wilma to train in a summer program for high school students who had the potential to be outstanding athletes. Wilma's parents allowed her to go.

The rest of Wilma's story includes world records, Olympic gold medals, and many honors. Wilma Rudolph's childhood disease could have caused her to give up on her dreams; instead, it became an obstacle that Wilma's courage, hard work, and determination overcame.

Think About It!

Give the correct answer.

*1. This type of story is _____. How do you know?
   a. a biography b. realistic fiction
2. What illness left Wilma Rudolph disabled?
3. What treatment helped strengthen Wilma's legs?
4. When did Wilma first start school?
5. What sport did Wilma play at first?
6. Why did Wilma join the track team?
   a. Her family thought it would be the best sport for her legs.
   b. It was her lifelong dream.
   c. She thought running would be fun.
7. What helped Wilma overcome her physical difficulty?

What Do YOU Think?

*Using God's Word, how might Wilma Rudolph's church family have encouraged her?

Character Theme

determination

Those who have trusted Christ as their Savior are never alone. God promises in His Word that He will never leave you or forsake you. Remembering this Bible truth helps Christians overcome the most difficult circumstances in life with victory. Remember this and other passages from God's Word when you need encouragement and determination.

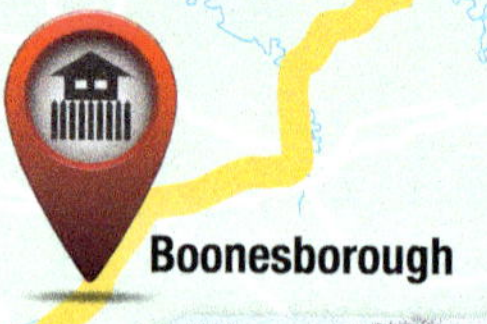

The Jacksons take an exciting tour of Fort Boonesborough and discover what it was like for Daniel Boone and other pioneers to live in the Kentucky wilderness in the 1700s.

Daniel Boone's Daughter

Aileen Fisher

Daniel Boone was an early American frontiersman and legendary hero, known for his settlement in Kentucky called Fort Boonesborough. The following selection is a fictional retelling based on historical records and an entry in Daniel Boone's own journal. Because Native Americans were called "Indians" at this time in history, he referred to them as such in his writings.

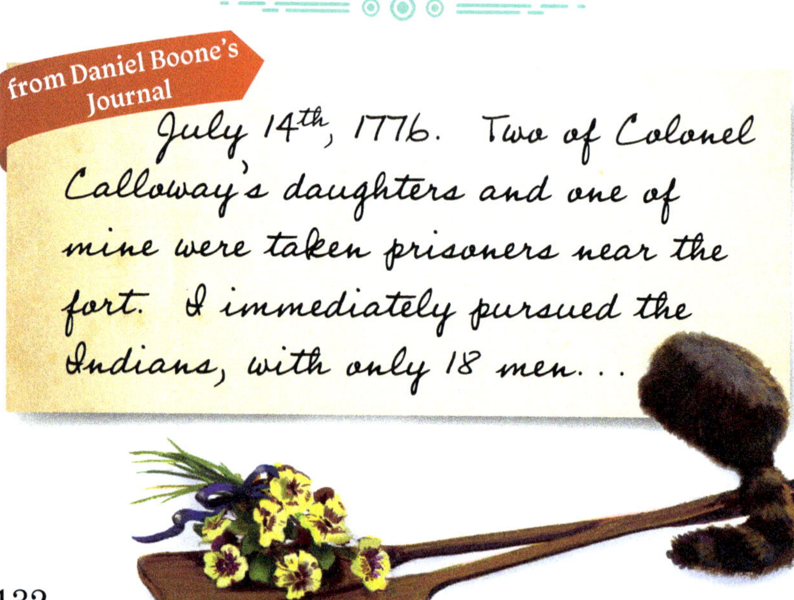

from Daniel Boone's Journal

July 14th, 1776. Two of Colonel Calloway's daughters and one of mine were taken prisoners near the fort. I immediately pursued the Indians, with only 18 men. . .

The five Indians hurried their captives along the narrow forest trail. Only one of the five could speak any English. "Walk fast," he told the three frightened girls. "Walk fast. No make trouble."

Jemima Boone blinked back her tears, trying not to cry. But with every step, they were getting farther away from the safety of the little log cabins at Fort Boonesborough, farther away from rescue.

Jemima wondered if anyone back at the fort had missed them yet. Had they guessed what had happened?

A choking sob drifted back to Jemima from her best friend, Frances Calloway. For all her bragging earlier that afternoon, Frances was scared to pieces, now. And Betsy Calloway was scared, too, even though she was much older than Frances and Jemima.

Betsy was sixteen, already. She should have known better. Yet she was the one who'd suggested the whole thing. "Let's take the canoe and paddle up around the bend," she'd said. Since Betsy knew a lot about handling a canoe, Jemima and Frances hadn't hesitated.

No, Jemima had not hesitated. But in her heart, she was sure that her father would have said, "You stay at the fort, Jemima. The river's no place for girls."

Jemima sighed, now. Her legs were becoming tired from hurrying so, and her heart was aching from fear and regret. If only they'd been satisfied with a brief paddle in the canoe! If only they'd had sense enough to turn back before ending up in trouble!

But once Frances had seen those pretty flowers growing on the north bank, there was no way to talk her out of picking them.

All Jemima's objections had been brushed off. "There may be Indians on the north bank!" she had said.

"Silly," Betsy had replied. "Indians so close to the fort? We haven't seen any Indians around the fort for months and months!"

And then Frances had said, "I'm surprised at you, Jemima. Imagine Daniel Boone's daughter being such a scared-y-cat!"

But now Jemima was sorry that she had let Frances and Betsy talk her into doing what she knew was wrong.

If there was one thing she had learned from her father, it was a healthy respect for the Indians.

Daniel Boone knew the Indians hated the white settlers because, as they moved West, they kept pushing the Indians from their own hunting grounds. And his understanding of the Indians made him realize how dangerous they could be, so he never took chances with them.

He had warned Jemima not to take chances, either. But steering their canoe close to the north bank to pick flowers this afternoon had been taking a chance. Suddenly they had discovered that they were stuck on a sand bar, just off shore.

And before they could push their canoe loose, hands had reached out from behind the canebrake[1] on the shore to seize them. They were Indian hands, Shawnee hands, the same hands that were urging them along the trail now, farther and farther from Fort Boonesborough.

Each weary mile that they walked took them deeper into Indian Country. And Jemima realized that if the Shawnees once got them beyond the Ohio River, even her father would not be able to find them.

Jemima quivered with fear as she thought about it. But this was no time to be afraid. She must keep her eyes open every moment, and not miss a chance to outsmart the Indians.

"Walk fast," growled the Indian behind her. Then, as if he were reading her thoughts, he added, "No trouble."

Jemima knew what he meant by "no trouble." He meant not to leave any signs that would show a rescue party which way they had come.

But that kind of "trouble" was the only hope for Jemima and her friends. And she was delighted, a moment later, to notice a fat brown mushroom at the side of the trail up ahead. If only she could kick off one corner of it.

---

[1] canebrake—*a thick growth of cane plants*

She stared up at the trees as she walked, so the Indians wouldn't guess what she had in mind. A piece of broken mushroom would be a perfect trail marker for her father and the rescue party!

The thought of her father gave Jemima new courage. In a low, firm voice, she said to Frances, who was still sobbing, "Don't be so worried, Frances. My father will be able to find us, no matter how far we go."

"But how can he?" Frances choked. "We've been crossing and recrossing our tracks in the cane-brake. And then they made us wade up that creek a long way . . ."

"He will find us," insisted Jemima. And she herself was surprised at how convincing her voice sounded. Listening to her own words seemed to strengthen her belief in what she was saying. "Don't worry, Frances," she repeated. "He'll find us, all right."

"Stop talk," the Indian demanded, moving closer. "No talk. Understand?"

Jemima sighed. Maybe he could make her stop talking, but he could not make her stop trying to leave a trail. As she walked along, Jemima secretly

worked loose a long blue thread from her dress, and dropped it behind her on a bush.

It was getting darker in the woods now. And she was glad of that.

Jemima knew it was not too dark for the Indians to follow their own forest trails. But she knew it was too dark for them to watch every movement of her hands and feet. An overturned stone, torn threads from her clothing, a broken twig—these would make the trail an open book for Daniel Boone to read.

The Indians hurried their captives along at a dogtrot.[2] At an open place on a high bank above the creek, the spokesman said, "We stop. Too dark."

The Indians tied the girls to some trees at the edge of the clearing. Then they took out their food pouches. They built no campfire.

Indians and captives alike received their share of the dried corn and dried meat that the Indians had brought with them.

"Sun-up, we go," said the Indian. "Now, all sleep."

Leaning up against the tree trunk, Jemima stretched out her tired legs and did her best to comfort Frances and Betsy.

"They'll find us tomorrow," Jemima whispered bravely.

"How?" groaned Frances. "We had a three- or four-hour start, maybe more."

---

[2] dogtrot—*a steady jog like the trot of a dog*

"My father will find us," Jemima whispered back. "I'm *sure* he will."

"How will he know which way to go?"

"He'll find our trail, somehow," replied Jemima. "You'll see. Don't worry. Now let's try to get some sleep."

Next day the Indians drove the girls along even harder. They made them backtrack and follow stream beds, keeping a constant watch on all of them. Once when Jemima "stumbled" on a root, displacing a stone, they carefully put it back in place and covered all signs of the fall.

Still, Jemima managed to drop bits of cloth and pieces of thread here and there.

But they were getting nearer and nearer to the Ohio River, farther and farther from Fort Boonesborough! Jemima decided to try something else to gain time.

She pretended to start crying. As soon as the Indian was within hearing distance, she sobbed loudly, "Father won't *ever* be able to find us! He's probably still wandering back in that first canebrake."

The Indian laughed. "No find, huh?" He spoke to the other Shawnees. They laughed, too. "Too bad. No find."

Jemima flung herself upon the ground, still putting on a great show of tears. "I'm so tired, I can't walk another step. I can't! I can't!"

“Anything to gain time,” she said to Frances under her breath.

“It won’t do any good,” groaned Frances. “They won’t find us, no matter how much time you gain!”

But after that, the Indians did not make their three captives go along so fast. They seemed to be convinced that no one, not even Daniel Boone, could follow the trail.

Noticing that the Indians were not watching them quite so closely, Jemima left more and more markers on the trail.

Toward evening, one of the men shot a deer, and they made a fire to cook it. The girls, tied to trees nearby, watched anxiously.

The Indians were working busily near the campfire when, suddenly, shots rang out.

Jemima screamed, “Father! Father!” And Frances started to cry, but not from fear this time. As the Indians leaped for the safety of the woods, Daniel Boone stepped from behind a tree, his gun smoking. Mr. Calloway and the rest of the rescue party followed him.

Jemima felt her father’s strong arms hugging her tight. Then he untied the strips of deerskin which held her to the tree. “My poor little girl,” he said. “You must have been scared!”

“I was at first,” Jemima said. “But, you know, Father, when I saw how scared Frances was, everything changed. The more I tried to make her feel

better, the better I felt myself. It was as if my little bit of courage just kept growing and growing!"

"That's the way it is with courage," Daniel Boone said, "only not everybody finds that out." He studied his daughter seriously for a moment. Then his eyes began to twinkle.

"Speaking of finding things out, I've been wondering about something. Which one of you girls managed to break off the edge of that mushroom?"

from Daniel Boone's Journal

On the 16th, I overtook them and recovered the girls.

Think About It!

Give the correct answer.

*1. Was the main event in this story true? How do you know?

*2. This selection is most like a(n) _____.

a. allegory b. biography c. historical fiction

3. Number the events in the order they happened in the plot.

_____ Jemima marked the trail for her father to find them.

_____ The Shawnees captured the girls and led them away from Fort Boonesborough.

_____ Betsy, Frances, and Jemima paddled up the river in a canoe.

_____ The rescue party arrived and the Shawnees fled.

*4. What is the turning point in the plot? Draw a star beside the event to show which one is the climax.

Character Themes

resourcefulness, courage, encouragement

What did Jemima do to help her father find her?

What can we learn from Jemima about courage?

How can we encourage others?

1 Thessalonians 5:11 "Wherefore comfort yourselves together, and edify one another, even as also ye do."

1 Thessalonians 4:18 "Wherefore comfort one another with these words."

an artist's depiction

? What Do YOU Think?

*1. Why was a wall built around the entire fort?
   a. to keep the buildings from falling down
   b. to protect those living inside the fort
   c. to separate Boonesborough from other towns or villages

*2. Why were the four blockhouses in each corner of the fort taller than the other buildings?
   a. to block the sun's harmful rays
   b. to house larger families
   c. to serve as lookout towers

*3. Why were the doors to the homes only on the inside of the fort?
   a. anyone entering a house could be seen
   b. the fort was built too quickly
   c. more doors would weaken the structure of the fort

*4. Why was it important to have a garden inside the fort?
   a. the inside of the fort had the best soil
   b. they didn't have to walk far to the garden
   c. to have a safe place to plant and harvest food

A Great Camping Trip

Bethany Urbina

"Everybody out!" called Dad. "The sooner we unload the van and set up the tent, the sooner we can have some fun!"

Christy and Caleb gazed at the sparkling Lake Michigan water in the distance. They couldn't wait to get a closer look. Quickly and carefully, they helped to set up the camping supplies. Once everything was in order, Dad suggested they head down to the water and fish for their supper. Caleb and Christy hadn't been fishing before, but soon, with Dad's help, they each cast a line into the water. Mom sat nearby on the shore holding Cole and taking pictures.

"Isn't it beautiful here?" she said with a sigh. "I have always loved visiting the Great Lakes."

“Can anyone name all five of the Great Lakes?” Dad asked.

“Oh! I think I remember!” shouted Caleb.

“Quietly!” Dad hushed. “You don’t want to scare away the fish.”

“Lake Michigan, of course,” whispered Christy. “Lake Superior, Lake Ontario. . . .”

“Lake Huron and Lake Erie,” Caleb finished for her.

Just then Christy’s fishing pole began to bend. Dad rushed to help her reel in her catch, but while he was helping Christy, Caleb felt a tug on his line.

“Dad, what about me?” he called out. Dad couldn’t help but laugh and called back, “You can do it, son! Just pull your rod back and reel it in!”

Caleb pulled and reeled as hard as he could until he pulled up a fine trout.

“Not bad for first-timers!” Dad teased and hugged Caleb and Christy both.

That night around the campfire, the Jacksons ate their delicious catch and looked up at the stars. "I wonder what it must have been like to live here in the pioneer days," Caleb thought out loud.

"Well, you're getting a little taste of that life right now!" said Mom. "Fishing for your food, sleeping in a tent or under the stars, cooking over a fire—those things were all a part of a pioneer's life."

"And then when they found a place to live, they would cut down these tall trees and build homes out of logs," added Dad.

"I don't know if I could live that way!" said Christy. "It sounds hard!"

"I know I could!" said Caleb. "It sounds fun to me."

"I think you both could," said Mom. "I'm sure sometimes it was fun, and sometimes it was hard. Both of you are very hard workers, and you love to find adventure in new places. I think you would make fine pioneers."

Christy and Caleb giggled and smiled into the glowing fire as Dad hugged Mom and asked, "What about me?"

Think About It!

Give the correct answer.

1. Where did the Jackson family stop to camp?
2. How was camping similar to pioneer living?
3. How do you think Mom will answer Dad's question "What about me"?

Theme

enjoying family

When each member of a family focuses on demonstrating patience, kindness, and love toward one another, the result is joy. Every family can enjoy spending time together and create some wonderful, lasting memories by following some principles found in God's Word.

1 Corinthians 13:4 "Charity suffereth long, and is kind; charity envieth not; charity vaunteth not itself, is not puffed up."

Ephesians 5:21 "Submitting yourselves one to another in the fear of God."

Colossians 3:13 "Forbearing one another, and forgiving one another, if any man have a quarrel against any: even as Christ forgave you, so also do ye."

Love is a word, love is a thought, and love is an action. What actions do you see in these verses that you could imitate or avoid to show love to your family?

Great Lakes

Let's travel with the Jackson family as they explore the Great Lakes region of the United States. We'll visit a beautiful lighthouse, make a tasty treat, relive the past, compare sandy shores, and see some of the largest things ever made.

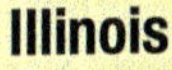

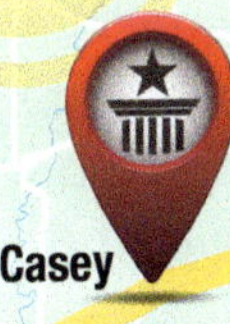
Casey

World's Largest Rocking Chair

Lake Michigan

While the Jacksons are in Illinois, they may want to stop and visit the town of Casey, where you can find a collection of some of the largest things ever made—like the world's largest rocking chair, a towering mailbox, and a huge wind chime. This wind chime measures 55 feet long and consists of five metal tubes that produce a strong, deep sound. You can even ring the chimes yourself! The designer of the wind chime also included within the frame the Christian fish and the Star of David; both represent aspects of the Christian faith.

"That's a crackerjack!"

Around the campfire, the Jacksons enjoy a favorite camping snack called Cracker Jack®. William Rueckheim and his brother Louis invented a snack consisting of popcorn and peanuts coated in a molasses-flavored caramel sauce. It was first produced and sold at the Chicago World's Fair in 1893. Legend says the caramel-coated popcorn got its name when, in 1896, a customer said after eating the snack, "That's a crackerjack!" Back then, that meant "It's good!" Cracker Jack® boxes are still sold at many Major League ballparks, including Wrigley Field in Chicago. During the "seventh-inning stretch," the fans in this stadium stand and sing "Take Me Out to the Ball Game," which contains a reference to the tasty Cracker Jack® snacks.

Follow the steps to make your own homemade treat.

Caramel-Coated Popcorn Recipe

Ingredients

- 4 quarts plain popped popcorn
- 1 cup salted peanuts (optional)
- 1 cup packed light brown sugar
- ½ cup butter
- ¼ cup light corn syrup
- ¼ teaspoon salt
- 1 teaspoon vanilla
- ½ teaspoon baking soda

Directions

First, place the popped popcorn in a large brown paper bag; set aside.

Next, combine brown sugar, butter, corn syrup, salt, and vanilla in a 2-quart glass dish.

Then, heat for 2 minutes in microwave. Remove and stir until well blended. Repeat this step and stir in the baking soda.

Next, pour the syrup over the popcorn in the paper bag. Fold down the top twice to close the bag, and shake vigorously to coat the popcorn.

Then, place the bag in the microwave and heat for 1 minute. Remove, shake, flip the bag over, and return it to the microwave.

Again, heat for another minute.

Then, pour the popcorn onto waxed paper and let cool until coating is set.

Finally, store in an airtight container.

Think It Through

Give the correct answer.

1. What text structure was used to write this recipe? Circle your answer(s) in the chart below.

Text Structures	
Narrative	Informative—nonfiction
Fiction	Descriptive
Nonfiction	Sequential

2. What would happen if you skipped the third step?
3. Is it possible to make this recipe by changing the order of directions?

Bill's Bill

Harry Stephen Keeler

For centuries people from all around the world have come to America for the opportunity to work hard and to be free to do what is right. You can find many of these hard-working people in big cities like Chicago. "Bill's Bill" is an inspirational story about a boy who learned an important lesson in honesty and hard work. Let's go back to the early 1900s and see what Bill's life was like.

Desire

Bill was a boy scout. He was a first-class scout too, and every scout knows what that means. He had stood many tests, but the one I am going to tell about was the severest[1] of all.

Bill longed with his whole heart for a motorcycle. After looking over all the motorcycles in the field, he decided that the Red Dart, which cost $190, was the machine for him. But the price! Only ten dollars less than two hundred—an

[1] severest—*most serious*

immense[2] sum, it seemed, for a boy of sixteen to save.

In the first place, Bill knew that he had no chance of getting help from his father, whose business was in anything but good condition. But Bill was not dismayed[3] by this fact; he decided to try to make money enough himself to buy that motorcycle. So he went to see Jerry O'Brien, the man who owned nearly all the newspaper routes on the north side of Chicago.

"Jerry," he said, "I have known several boys who carried papers for you. Can't you give me a job on one of the morning routes?"

Jerry looked at him some time before he spoke. "Well," he drawled,[4] "I do need a boy for the Dearborn Avenue route in the morning, and the Clark Street route in the afternoon. Each one pays a dollar a week. But think it over well, youngster. The morning route means that you've got to rise at half-past four, so as to start at five, and it will be nearly seven when you finish. The afternoon route will take from four to five-thirty. And don't forget it, either—it's cold these winter mornings. You go all the way from Chicago Avenue to North Avenue, which means you'll have to hustle. Think it over. I don't want to teach you the routes and then have you back out in a week or two."

---

[2]immense—*great in size; huge*
[3]dismayed—*discouraged*
[4]drawled—*spoke slowly with drawn-out words*

But Bill did not require much "thinking it over." The idea of owning a Red Dart made it seem easy to climb out of bed before daylight on winter mornings, wade through snowdrifts, and lose playtime after school.

"Take me, Jerry," he begged. "I won't back out. I want money for something that costs a lot—and the only way I can get it is to earn it."

Bill's father not only showed no opposition to the plan but even helped to reassure Mother because of her objections; so Bill reported to Jerry the next morning to be taught the route.

It was no soft snap.[5] In October, the mornings were warm and pleasant. As winter gradually crept nearer, however, all of the boy's willpower was needed to pull him out of bed into an ice-cold room. Shivering, he drew on his trousers, flannel shirt and two sweaters and made his way down the street, in the teeth of a driving gale or a sleety rain, to the alley where his stock of papers awaited him. The load was heavy enough when he started out with it, but, oddly enough, as it grew smaller it grew more leaden,[6] until by the end of the route it was almost as tiring as at the beginning.

The morning's work over, there followed in rapid succession[7] breakfast, school, homework, the afternoon route. By the time the afternoon papers were delivered, it was almost suppertime. After supper, it was early to bed with Bill, in order to get sufficient sleep for rising before daybreak next morning. That was the daily round, and no time whatever was left from Monday to Saturday for football, skating, or any of the other things which Bill delighted in.

There was this consolation,[8] however. Every day brought him just a little nearer to the longed-for motorcycle.

The last snow melted, and the warm spring mornings returned. Spring ran into summer, and

---

[5] soft snap—*simple task*
[6] leaden—*heavy and hard to move*
[7] succession—*coming after*
[8] consolation—*comfort*

summer turned out to be pleasanter, since Bill had plenty of time for baseball, swimming, and other joys, in spite of three and a half hours of carrying papers. But at last, only a few weeks remained before school would reopen and the grind would begin again—papers, school, papers, bed; papers, school, papers, bed!

Bill tried to keep this out of his mind as much as possible. He preferred to dwell on ninety dollars snugly laid away. One more year—or fifty weeks—and he would have another hundred dollars and the beautiful Red Dart.

A Find

Then came the astonishing event—the finding of the $100 bill. It happened in this fashion:

One evening, Bill saw in a paper a full-page advertisement of the Red Dart Motorcycle Company. It announced that the company had issued a new booklet, which would be given or mailed to anybody interested in motorcycles. Bill, being among those interested, walked all the way downtown the next afternoon to get one of the little books. After feasting his eyes on the wonderful display of motorcycles in the salesrooms, he asked for a booklet.

He opened it as he left the building. At that moment, he glanced down at the pavement and saw a folded slip moving in the wind. Bill stooped to pick it up, but the wind whirled it under a

wagon standing by the curb of the crowded street. Reaching out quickly, the boy seized the paper. It crackled upon unfolding. One long look—and Bill tingled from his head to his toes.

A hundred dollars!

No one in the passing crowd had paid him the least attention, though he felt that all Chicago was looking at him with a thousand eyes.

At last! Why, it made up the sum needed for the motorcycle! It saved fifty weeks of work.

As he trudged homeward, the boy's mind was in a whirl. Every now and then he drew the banknote from his pocket and read it, as though to make sure that what had happened was real and not a dream. What luck!

Then came other and different thoughts—troublesome thoughts. The loser might advertise. Bill knew that in such an event there was nothing to do but return the money. He might not see the advertisement, however. Or the owner might believe the bill to be lost beyond recovery and make no effort to regain it. In that case—

Struggle

All the time the boy was delivering the afternoon papers, he reasoned that if he did not look at the lost-and-found columns for several weeks, he would not see the advertisement, even if an advertisement were printed. In that case, he might buy the motorcycle without any stings of conscience. He could give up the newspaper routes, which left him no time for himself.

As Bill walked the street, a small voice urged him, "Don't look at the lost-and-found column; don't look at the lost-and-found column!"

Bill made more mistakes that afternoon than he had ever made before. Where he should have left copies of the *Evening News*, angry subscribers found the *Post*; and where *Posts* were desired, copies of the *Evening News* were left. Every now and then, Bill rested the bundle on his knee and felt his pocket, to make sure that the bill was still there. All the while his mind worked on the problem without rest. He thought that he must look at the lost-and-found column; then he felt that it would be very foolish to look. Should he have the motorcycle at once, without more work? Or should he throw away this splendid chance?

That night at supper Bill ate little. His mother noticed that something was troubling him. His father made no sign, however, that he had seen anything at all, but when his mother left the room, he spoke to the boy.

"Well, Bill," he asked, "are you worried because vacation is nearly over? Or has Jerry O'Brien decided to give your routes to another boy?"

"I am sorry that vacation is nearly over but—"

"But what?"

"Will you answer an imaginary question for me, Father?" asked the boy.

"Yes; what is it?"

"Well," Bill began slowly, "if you found something valuable—say money—would you look in the papers to see if it was advertised?"

"It is not polite to answer one question by asking another," his father replied, "but that is what I am going to do. Listen. My business is not very good at present, although I manage to keep you at school, and let you have for your own what money you make after school. Now if I lost some money—even a little—do you think that the finder should keep it or return it?"

"I suppose your question answers mine," Bill said solemnly. "When you lose anything, you feel that it ought to be returned; and when you find something, the loser feels the same way."

He went to bed without saying another word.

The next morning, Bill dressed early and tiptoed from the house. Fifteen minutes later he reached the point where he got his papers—half of them *Tribunes*, half of them *Heralds*.

For several minutes he stared at the papers. All that he had to do, he reflected, was to open one of them quickly, locate the lost-and-found column and run his eye down it. If he did so, he might come across the owner of the yellow $100 bill that he had hidden in the bureau[9] drawer. Then he would never be able to rest until he had restored[10] the money. Perhaps, after all, it was best that he should not look. If people were careless, it served them right to lose things. Surely it would be foolish to look. But on the other hand, the loser might be a bank messenger, who would have to make good the loss.

The boy raised the bunch of papers, swung his shoulder strap around it, and started out on his route. Whenever he rolled a paper before tossing it from the sidewalk to a porch, his hand paused for a second in the motion. But he always managed to throw the paper and go on to the next subscriber's house. Thus *Tribune* after *Tribune* and *Herald* after *Herald* left the bundle, until finally but one paper remained—a *Tribune*.

[9]bureau—*dresser*
[10]restore—*give back*

Victory

For some time, Bill hesitated in front of the last house on his route. Then he lifted the paper to throw it—without having looked at it. At that moment his eye fell on his scout badge, and the first scout law flashed through his mind: "A scout's honor is to be trusted." His arm fell slowly to his side. He seated himself on a doorstep and unfolded the paper.

There was the lost-and-found column. And a moment later his heart dropped down clean through to his shoes! His visions of a motorcycle, a beautiful, glittering Red Dart, vanished into thin air as he read this advertisement:

> **LOST:** Yesterday, a bill of large denomination;[11] owner can identify it by giving serial number; reasonable reward if returned between 7 and 9 p.m. to John Bennet, 1400 Lake Shore Drive.

Bill went home to breakfast. His heart was light—most happily light—although he was about to lose his treasure. He realized that the tussle[12] he had had with himself, when he held the last *Tribune*, had been a hard one. But, after all, he would not now have that money on his conscience. The coming year could not pass more slowly than the one just closed, and at its end he would have the Red Dart anyway, all paid for by the sweat of his brow. And perhaps the reward for the return of the bill would help a little.

[11] denomination—*value*
[12] tussle—*struggle*

At seven o'clock that evening Bill was on Lake Shore Drive. In a few minutes he had found "1400." He was rather surprised to see a splendid mansion, with a well-kept lawn, a driveway, and other evidences of wealth. After fumbling nervously for a moment at the iron gate, the boy picked up courage enough to walk up the steps and ring the bell. A man in a gray uniform answered the summons.[13]

"I would like—I would like to speak to Mr. John Bennet," Bill said.

"Step this way," said the butler. "Stand here; I will see if he is busy."

The butler knocked at a door at the end of the hall. It opened slightly. As it opened, Bill caught sight of a little sharp-featured man, with iron-gray hair and small piercing eyes.

"Boy to see you, sir," explained the butler.

"Tell him to come in," said the little man.

Bill did so. Mr. Bennet closed the door.

"Sit down," he invited. "What can I do for you?"

"I have found your money," Bill blurted out.

"Humph!" returned Mr. Bennet. "So you found it?" He paused. "Well, I lost it and my wife inserted the advertisement. She has an old-fashioned notion that everybody is honest. It's all nonsense! I lost a hundred dollar bill. Was that what you found?"

"Yes," Bill answered. "You said in your advertisement that you knew the number. If it's the same number that's on the bill, I will hand you the money."

---

 [13]summons—*a call to come*

The little man jerked a notebook from his pocket. He thumbed the leaves a moment.

"Always put down the numbers of big bills, boy," he said. "This is what I always do. It pays in case they get lost. Let me see—here it is. Number M17472447, Series 1902."

"It's your money, then," interrupted Bill.

He laid the crisp yellow note in Mr. Bennet's hand.

"Humph! Humph!" snorted Mr. Bennet, staring at Bill as if he were some rare curiosity. "How did you happen to find it? Where did you come across it? What time of day was it? Where do you live? Do you work downtown? What is your name?"

The torrent[14] of questions took away Bill's breath. Then he collected his wits.[15]

[14]torrent—*a rushing flow*
[15]wits—*ability to think and understand*

"I go to school," he answered. "My name is William Carston, and I live at 124 West Center Street. I happened to go downtown yesterday to get a Red Dart motorcycle advertisement—I have been saving money a long time for a Red Dart. When I came out of the Red Dart office on Madison Street, I looked down and saw the bill, and—"

"Motorcycle!" exploded Mr. Bennet. "Motorcycle! It's all nonsense! Do you want to get blown over the moon? I wouldn't ride one of the pesky things for a million dollars. It's all nonsense! Why, if I—"

He was interrupted by a rapping on the door. Mr. Bennet opened it, and the butler said, "Mr. Smith from New York to see you, sir."

With a quick motion of his wrist, Mr. Bennet jerked out his watch and snapped it open.

"Hm-hm-hm!" he mumbled. "Forgot all about my appointment with Smith. Hawkins, show this young gentleman out."

A big figure loomed up behind the butler.

"Is that you, Smith? I forgot all about you. Step in," said Mr. Bennet.

Bill found himself conducted[16] through the hall and heard the door close behind him. He recovered himself as he walked down the cement path to the sidewalk.

"Well, where's the reward?" he said. "If it had been anybody but a millionaire—"

[16] conducted—*led*

Presently, however, as he walked along homeward, he found his disappointment lightening. A feeling of great relief was coming over him. He was glad to have the bill off his hands.

Surprise

The next morning, Bill came into the dining room with a bright face. His mother and father looked at him with curiosity.

"Letter for you, Bill," said his father.

Bill wonderingly tore open the envelope. At first he saw nothing inside; then he found a small white card in one corner. Taking it out, he read with perplexity[17] the words written in red ink on one side:

JOHN C. BENNET
Owner and General Manager
Red Dart Motorcycle Co.
CHICAGO NEW YORK LONDON

Quickly he turned the card over. The printed words on the other side read:

Sales Department:
Credit bearer with $100
on purchase of any
motorcycle in stock.
J. B.

[17] perplexity—*state of being confused*

That afternoon, the proudest and happiest boy in Chicago came home with the finest motorcycle in the whole world.

Think About It!

Give the correct answer.

1. What things did Bill need to consider before accepting the paper route job?

*2. Why did the load of papers seem heavier at the end of the route?

3. Though Bill had to work very hard and had little time to play, what was his consolation?

4. Why did Bill make so many mistakes after finding the money? What was bothering him?

*5. Which of the following best explains the theme of the story?

   a. Hard work pays off.

   b. Honesty is the best policy.

   c. Never give up.

Character Themes

honesty, hard work, self-discipline

Anyone who determines to work hard is going to face difficulties. What obstacles did Bill face when he began his new job?

What helped Bill make the right decision?

If you were in Bill's place, what would you do?

Acts 24:16 "And herein do I exercise myself, to have always a conscience void of offense toward God, and toward men."

On our road trip east, let's use our imaginations and enjoy more of the great outdoors at Potato Falls in Copper Falls State Park, Wisconsin.

A Friend in Sable

Savannah Patrick

Dawn broke lazily through the misty forest. Birds twittered. Leaves glistened from an early morning shower. The sun beamed through Rosie's hollow log on the forest floor, highlighting the black and white fur mask surrounding her eyes. She squinted grumpily and frowned. Rosie hated mornings, and *this* morning felt even worse since her scavenging last night had produced very little food. She rolled over, grunted, and tried to go back to sleep, but then her stomach grumbled loudly. She gave a frustrated sigh, stretched her arms upward, and yawned.

"I guess a bit of breakfast will do me good," she thought. Rosie trudged out of her log, wiping the sleep from her eyes as she went.

"Good morning, Rosie!" Red twittered as he scratched about for a fat worm. Rosie forced a smile and waved without answer.

"Rosie! How was the hunt last night?" Sarge called out as he spiraled down his tree and began digging for an acorn he had hidden last week.

"It could have been better," Rosie replied gloomily. "I'm still awfully hungry."

"You're in luck, neighbor!" said Sarge. "I found a berry bush just over the ridge that way." He pointed in the direction of the bush. Rosie raised a paw in thanks, turned, and began walking toward the ridge, stretching her mouth wide again in a huge yawn. Suddenly, Sarge called, "Rosie, look out!"

But it was too late. Before she could stop herself, Rosie stumbled into a low-hanging spider web, catching a bit of the sticky stuff in her mouth. Startled, she spat and wiped her paws wildly across her lips and tongue, trying to clear her muzzle of the stringy web. Then she glanced upward, now in quite a foul temper, to see the cause of this unpleasant encounter.

Strung between the fork of a low-hanging twig was an intricate web, and in the center of that web sat Sable the spider, waving pleasantly to Rosie with one of her long, spindly arms.

"Morning, neighbor," Sable said pleasantly in her small, silky voice. "Sorry about your muzzle, but you've really got to start watching where you're going. That's the third time this week!"

Rosie gave a humph in return. Of all her woodland neighbors, Rosie thought that Sable was the most disagreeable. She never washed her food before she ate it, her table manners were deplorable[1] (she was always slurping flies loudly), and worst of all, she built her webs in the most inconvenient places. Rosie was sick of it. She was finished being neighborly. Sable was her friend no longer.

"That does it!" Rosie cried. "You're going to have to live somewhere else. I can't be a neighbor to such a sloppy creature anymore, Sable!" With that, Rosie hastily snapped Sable's twig from the tree, holding the web away from her face. The other animals gasped. Sable had never done anyone any

[1] deplorable—*wretched; terribly bad*

harm. Her webs were easily avoidable, and she even kept the insect population comfortably low for the neighborhood.

It was Oliver who spoke up. He was known for his wisdom, and the other animals of the forest often looked to him for advice. "Now, now, Rosie, we know you've had a bad morning, but that's no way to treat a neighbor. If anyone is being disagreeable right now, it's you. I think Sable deserves an apology. Who-o-o agrees?" Red and Sarge nodded silently.

Rosie pursed[2] her lips in thought. Oliver was right. Rosie shouldn't have let her rough night affect her mood so. She sighed and opened her mouth to speak. But Sable interrupted in a quiet voice.

"No, no, don't apologize, Rosie. I never realized you felt that way about me. If that's truly how you feel, I will move away. I've heard there are plenty of tasty bugs to eat in the Potato River neighborhood, and the views at Potato Falls will be a nice change. This neighborhood will be better without me anyway." The spider dropped daintily to the ground and began making her way toward her new home.

The animals were shocked and silent. They looked at Rosie expectantly. Rosie hung her shoulders and let the twig fall from her paw. She didn't want to say anything. She just wanted to forget

[2]pursed—*puckered*

about this whole, awful morning. Without eating breakfast, she crawled slowly back into her log, curled up, and went to sleep. She had lost her appetite.

The days and nights passed slowly. Rosie thought that things would simply go back to normal, but she just couldn't stop thinking about Sable. All the animals missed her. Red often recalled how Sable had shared the insects she caught in her web if he was passing by. Sarge missed her greeting him every morning—they had shared the same tree. Rosie even admitted missing the way the dew glistened beautifully on Sable's delicate web. In the nighttime hours, Oliver often told Rosie the history of the Spider family and what a great asset they were to the forest.

"You'll see very soon; our neighborhood will be quite miserable without our little spider friend."

And Rosie *did* notice a big change in the neighborhood. Slowly but surely, hundreds of insects moved in with the woodland creatures. At first, Red and Rosie welcomed this change, since creepy crawlies made up a good part of their diet. But before long, the large swarms of gnats and flies became too much for everyone. There was constant swatting, flicking, scratching, and itching. Very soon, *everyone* wanted to leave the neighborhood. It had become a most unpleasant place to reside.

Early one morning as everyone slept, Rosie stopped her scavenging at the berry bush to swat the gnats that buzzed around her eyes. "What a mess I've made of things," she thought. "I guess there's nothing to do now but to fix it. I will go to Potato Falls and find Sable right now. I will say I'm sorry, and I will bring her back." Leaving her delicious snack, she shambled[3] away from her home and into the quiet forest, calling to Sable all the while.

[3] shambled—*shuffled*

Finally, after hours of wandering, Rosie heard the sound of rushing water in the distance. The waterfall had to be close. She called even louder as she came nearer to the thundering falls. Then, nearly muted by the rushing water, a faint cry came to Rosie's ears. She moved closer to the tiny voice and saw, strung between two leaves and gleaming in the sunlight, a magnificent spider web. And there on the web was Sable, graceful and kind as always, waving in greeting.

"Oh, Sable!" Rosie called excitedly, wiping a tear from her whiskers, "I thought I'd never find you." Then words began to gush like a spring from her mouth. "It's been so lonely without you, and the insects are overrunning everything, and I didn't mean what I said about you, and I'm very sorry for being such a disagreeable neighbor, and we all want you to come back home, *please*!"

Sable chuckled. "Oh Rosie, I've missed everyone too—you especially!"

"Do you forgive me," asked Rosie, "even after how unkind I've been to you?"

"I do forgive you, and I will come home. Potato Falls is a lovely neighborhood, but I do miss my friends dearly. It sounds like a feast is waiting for me there, too!"

Rosie laughed. "Oh, thank you! Thank you! I'll take you home. You can even ride here between my ears."

The warmth of the sun stirred Sarge from his slumbering. He opened his eyes lazily, and as his eyes adjusted to the brightness, he saw something flash like diamonds in the sunlight. "Almost looks like Sable's old spider web," he thought absently. Then his eyes flashed open in recognition, and he saw it. It *was* Sable's spider web, only it was higher in the tree than usual—higher than a raccoon's mouth could reach, he noted—and there was Sable, his neighbor, waving to him just as she always did. He scampered down the tree from branch to branch until he reached her.

"Sable! Where did you . . . ? How did you . . . ?" But he couldn't seem to finish his thoughts. His mind was racing.

"Sshh," whispered the spider, "you'll wake her." Sable pointed down to Rosie's hollow log. A pair of raccoon feet projected carelessly from the den, and the sound of contented snores echoed from the opening. "She traveled through the forest from Potato Falls to bring me back. We only just arrived about an hour ago."

Sarge grinned and shook his head. "I can hardly believe it! Welcome back, neighbor. The forest just wasn't the same without you."

Think About It!

Give the correct answer.

1. This story is _____. Explain your answer.
   a. historical fiction
   b. narrative fiction
   c. narrative nonfiction
2. Describe the setting at the beginning of the story.
3. What was Rosie doing before she ran into Sable's web?
4. How did the other animals feel about the way Rosie treated Sable?

*5. Fill in the effects for the cause.

Cause Because Rosie moved Sable and her web away from the neighborhood,

Effect ______________________________

____

____

Effect ______________________________

____

____

Cause Because Rosie apologized for being disagreeable,

Effect ______________________________

____

____

What Do YOU Think?

* How could Rosie's problem at the beginning of the story have been avoided?

To BUILD ON IT, see page 197.

Michigan

As the Jacksons head north, they will enjoy a hike across a beautiful three-way wooden footbridge in Midland, Michigan, known as the Tridge. Why do you think it is called a "tridge"?

Little Gray Shoes

from *In Grandma's Attic* by Arleta Richardson

The winter I was six years old, I had diphtheria.[1] After a few weeks, when I began to feel a little better, Grandma brought the basket to my bed. Most everything in Grandma's house had a story, but the basket was full of them!

The basket contained buttons . . . all sizes, shapes, colors, and kinds. There were so many things to do with them, that it was hard to know how to start. Should I sort out all the round buttons? Or string the red buttons all together? Or maybe see how many different shapes there were? I seemed never to get to the end of the possibilities.

On this day, as I dug to the bottom of the basket, my fingers felt a new shape—one I hadn't noticed before. I brought the button out and looked at

[1] diphtheria—*a rare infectious disease*

it curiously. It was a small silver-gray triangle. It had no holes through it, nor a hook on the back. There seemed to be no way to sew it on anything.

"Grandma," I called. "Here's a button I never saw before. Where did it come from?"

Grandma came to look. She turned the button over in her hand thoughtfully.

"Why, this was one of my shoe buttons," she replied.

"Shoe button?" I asked. "Did you wear shoes with buttons on them? How was the button fastened on?"

"Oh, yes," said Grandma, "my shoes had buttons all the way up the side. The little hook that held this button came off long ago. I guess this is the only one that hasn't been lost."

Grandma continued to turn the button over in her hand. Her eye had the faraway look of a story, so I settled back on the pillows and waited.

"These were the most beautiful shoes I had ever seen," Grandma began. "We only had one new pair a year, and it was very important to make a good choice. Ma took me into town in September to shop for my new shoes. The first pair the man brought out were these wonderful gray shoes with silver triangle buttons. They were soft doe-skin,[2] and to me, there had never been anything so lovely.

"'Oh, Ma,' I said. 'These are the ones I want. I don't even want to look at any others.'

"'Well, try them on,' said Ma. 'We'll see.'

"The man put the shoes on my feet and buttoned them up with a tiny buttonhook. I held my feet straight out in front of me and admired those shoes. Oh, such beauty!

"'Stand up,' said Ma. 'See if they are going to be too short.'

"Too short! Of course they weren't. They couldn't be. But when I stood down on the floor, my toes touched the end of the shoes.

"'Do they pinch?' asked the man.

"'Oh, no, they don't pinch! They are just fine!' I hastened to reassure them.

"But Ma was doubtful.

"'Remember,' she said. 'You have to wear these all year. It doesn't look like there is much room to grow. Do you have them in the next size?' she asked.

---

[2] doe-skin—*soft leather made from the skin of a deer or lamb*

"He didn't. All he had in the next size was a pair of black shoes with shiny patent leather toes and small round buttons. The thought of leaving those wonderful gray shoes was more than I could stand.

"'These are just fine, Ma,' I protested. 'These fit just fine. They don't hurt a bit.'

"A little twinge[3] told me that the shoes really were too small, and that I should tell Ma that my toes touched the end. But my desire to have a beautiful pair of shoes to show Sarah Jane and the other girls won out, and I said nothing.

"Ma paid for the shoes, and they were wrapped for me to carry home in triumph. I wore them to church the following Sunday, and modestly accepted the admiration of my friends.

---

[3]twinge—*a sudden feeling of emotional pain*

"For a few weeks, the shoes only felt a little tight. Then as my feet continued to grow, they really began to pinch. Of course, I could say nothing to Ma. I could not admit that I had stretched the truth to get them and anyway, there was no money to replace them. Finally I found that I could only wear the shoes when I was sitting down, so that I could curl my toes up inside. On Sunday morning, I would pull my boots on over my heavy stockings and carefully conceal my shoes under my cape until we got to church. Then I would sit through the long service with my poor feet aching in those beautiful shoes.

The day came, as I knew it would, when I could not get the shoes on at all. Ma had to be told. With much sobbing, I admitted that I had been deceitful about the shoes. Now it was only early in December, and I had no shoes to wear for the remainder of the winter.

"Ma was sorry, not only that the shoes no longer fit, but that her little girl had deceived her. Oh, what I would have given for those homely black shoes that would fit! But that was impossible. There was no money for more shoes. The only solution was a pair of my older brother's outgrown shoes.

"Pa tried his best to shine them up for me, but they were boy's shoes! And they had metal toes! I would never leave the house again. I would just stay home until it was time to go barefoot in the spring. But of course I didn't. Although I cried huge tears over them, I wore Roy's shoes to church. I did my best to hide my feet under the bench so no one would see, but such things are not easy to hide.

"When Christmas came, I was delighted to see among my gifts a new rag doll that Ma had made and wrapped in a knitted shawl. But when I pulled back the shawl, what should look up at me but two gray shoe-button eyes! I looked quickly at Ma, but she acted as though nothing was wrong. I looked again at the doll. Her smiling mouth was not really laughing at me, I decided. In fact, she looked quite sympathetic. I touched the little buttons and thought how foolish I had been. This little doll would remind me to think twice before I did a deceitful thing like that again!

"My gray-eyed Emily was my companion until I was too old for dolls. There were others, even one with a china head, but none so dear as Emily with her kind smile and shoe-button eyes."

Grandma dropped the button into the basket and went back to her work. I dozed off thinking of the little gray shoes, and Grandma, a little girl just like me.

Think About It!

Give the correct answer.

1. From whose point of view is this story written? How do you know?
2. What reminded Grandma of the story of her shoes?
3. What was the problem with the gray shoes?
4. What was the result of Grandma not telling the whole truth about the shoes?
5. What gift did Grandma receive for Christmas that reminded her of the gray shoes?
6. What was special about the gift?

*7. What lesson did Arleta learn from Grandma's gray shoes?

Character Themes

contentment, honor, honesty

Arleta's grandma saw something she wanted so badly she did whatever she could do to gain it. Would you have done it differently?

Where should you go for help in making the right choices in your life?

Hebrews 13:5 "Let your conversation be without covetousness; and be content with such things as ye have: for He hath said, I will never leave thee, nor forsake thee."

Which Is Which?

Kayla Sanders

The United States of America is a very unique place because it is home to multiple ecosystems.[1] You can find deserts in Arizona, marshes in Louisiana, and tropical jungles in Hawaii. There is so much variety! Some ecosystems are very similar, and others are very different. Let's look at the similarities and differences found between the Great Lakes and the Gulf of Mexico.

The Great Lakes are made up of five separate bodies of fresh water: Lake Huron, Lake Ontario, Lake Michigan, Lake Erie, and Lake Superior. You can find the Great Lakes stretched across the U.S. northern border, touching many states as well as the country of Canada. Unlike the Great Lakes, the Gulf of Mexico is a warm body of salt water, part of the Atlantic Ocean, to the South of the United States. It touches several southern states, eastern Mexico, and extends to the island of Cuba.

[1] ecosystem—*a community of organisms, such as plants and animals, interacting with their physical environment*

Because these two regions are on opposite sides of the eastern United States, their climates are very different. If you learn more about each climate, you can prepare for a visit to each region. In the Great Lakes area, it is normal to still feel crisp, cool air during summer months. A light jacket would be appropriate for the cooler, breezy evenings. On the other hand, the Gulf is known for its bright sun and hot, sticky air, full of humidity. Knowing more about the heat will encourage you to bring sunscreen and drink plenty of water.

Differences in climates invite differences in severe weather—like hurricanes and blizzards. Between the months of June and November, the warm waters in the Gulf of Mexico can attract hurricanes. If a hurricane does reach land, the damage from wind and flooding can be severe. Although the Great Lakes do not experience hurricanes, most states bordering the lakes endure heavy snowfall. In some areas, snow can fall as early as October and as late as May. The Great Lakes are infamous[2] for lake-effect snow. This snow is the result of water

[2]infamous—*bad reputation*

evaporation filling the clouds quickly and creating heavy snowfall in a small amount of time.

Both the Great Lakes and the Gulf of Mexico are known for some of the most beautiful beaches in the country. Down south, Florida's sugar-white sands and emerald-colored waters bring thousands of tourists throughout the year. Beachgoers enjoy shelling—collecting a variety of interesting seashells with unique patterns and designs. However, some of America's best rock hunting happens along the northern lakeshores. Unusual-looking rocks are polished and used to make beautiful jewelry and other decorations.

Northerners and southerners alike enjoy recreational[3] fishing during their free time. Both regions are well known for the sport as well as the food they produce.

If you go on vacation to either region, don't forget to catch a birds-eye view of each of the coasts. You can do this by taking a tour of one of the many lighthouses you are sure to find!

The Great Lakes and the Gulf of Mexico are different in many ways, but they have things

[3] recreational—*hobby; sport*

in common. Looking at similarities and differences between the two ecosystems helps us understand and appreciate particular places in the amazing world that God has created for us to enjoy!

Think It Through

Give the correct answer.

1. What is the main idea of this selection?
2. Underline these signal words in the selection that help you identify the text structure.

similar	different	similarities	differences
unlike	on the other hand	although	both
however	alike	either	in common

3. Fill in the blanks to compare and contrast the Great Lakes and the Gulf of Mexico.

The Great Lakes	Features	Gulf of Mexico
	location	
	water	
	bodies of water	
	climate	
	severe weather	
	hobbies	

 To BUILD ON IT, see page 198.

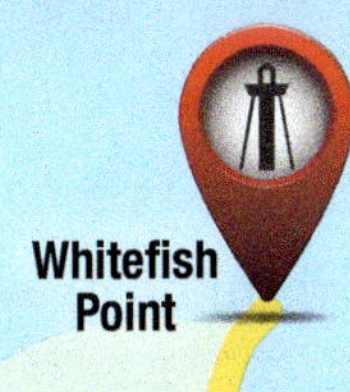

Whitefish Point

Michigan

The Jacksons' last stop on their road trip east is Whitefish Point on Lake Superior in the Upper Peninsula of Michigan. Known as the Graveyard of Ships, it is a favorite spot for scuba divers to explore sunken ships, finding them preserved[1] up to 170 years by the lake's cold water.

Today, ship captains can navigate[2] Lake Superior and know they can trust the Whitefish Point lighthouse to guide them safely across.

Jesus— Our Lighthouse

Kayla Sanders

Lighthouses, like the one at Whitefish Point in Michigan, have two jobs. The first is to warn ships of dangerous places, like shallow water or rocky shorelines. The second is to guide ships safely to shore during a storm.

While the lighthouse stands tall on the shore, it cannot prevent storms from coming. The very sight

[1] preserved—*kept in the same condition*
[2] navigate—*direct a vessel on its course*

of the lighthouse is a comfort to a sailor when there are signs of danger or when he cannot see what lies ahead.

For centuries, people have thought of the lighthouse as a symbol of guidance and instruction. How does what you know about a lighthouse compare to what you know about God in His Word?

In John 8:12 Jesus said, "I am the light of the world: he that followeth Me shall not walk in darkness, but shall have the light of life." Jesus spent His life on Earth inviting all to come to Him and follow Him.

Much like the sailor, the Christian is on a voyage. Whether he faces dangers or simply needs to make decisions for the future, he trusts God's Word for guidance and direction. The examples we find within the Bible give us the light we need to keep us from danger and give us daily direction.

Think About It!

Give the correct answer.

*1. What does the lighthouse symbolize?

*2. How is Jesus compared to a lighthouse?

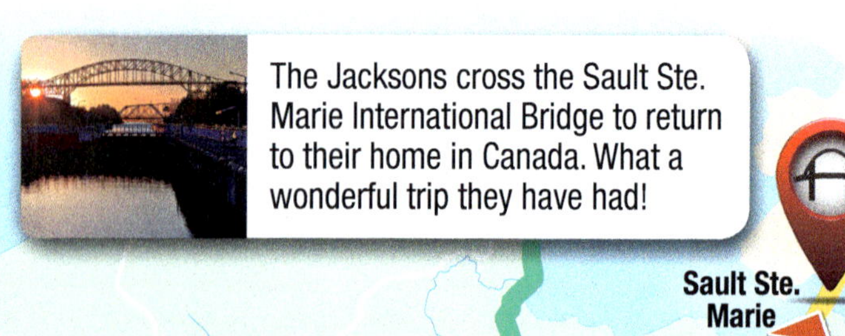

What Do YOU Think?

What are your favorite memories from the Jacksons' Road Trip East?

The Little Road

Nancy Byrd Turner

A little road was straying
Across a little hill.
I asked, "May I go with you, Road?"
It answered, "If you will."

'Twas travel-stained and shabby,
And dust was on its face.
Said I: "How fine to wander free
To every lovely place!

"Or, if you're off to mountains
Or if you're off to sea,
Or if you're bound across the world,
It's all the same to me."

We loitered[1] in the sunlight,
We journeyed on together;
The sky was like a bluebird's wing,
The wind was like a feather.

---

[1] loiter—*to remain still without any real purpose*

We passed a ruddy[2] robin
    Who called, "How do you do?"
Some daisies shook their bonnets back
    And begged, "Ah, take us too!"

A squirrel briefly joined us,
    A brook came hurrying down;
We wandered through a meadow green
    And by a busy town.

When dusky twilight met us,
    No feet so slow as mine.
"Why, there's a little house," I said,
    "With windows all ashine.

"Perhaps, since night is nearing,
    I'd rather rest than roam."
"I knew you would," said Little Road;
    "That's why I brought you home."

[2]ruddy—*reddish in color*

Think About It!

Give the correct answer.

*1. What did the narrator ask the road in the first stanza?

*2. Underline the similes in the fourth stanza.

*3. What time of day is it in the last two stanzas? How do you know?

*4. How did the road take the narrator home?

Write a Rhyming Poem

Complete after "The Last Word of a Bluebird" on page 9.

Using descriptive details like Robert Frost, write a short poem with pairs of rhyming words.

Creative Collaboration

Complete after "The Middle Bear" on page 20.

What Would YOU Do?

Grandma and Grandpa are coming to a special performance that you are participating in, but they don't know how to get from their car to the location of your performance. Collaborate with others to write up a route that includes directions from the car to your "stage." Draw a map in the box below that matches the directions you wrote.

Cause and Effect— Problem and Solution

Complete after "Little Georgie Sings a Song" on page 39.

Notice the cause for Little Georgie's trouble. Fill in the effect, the problem it caused, and the solution to his problem.

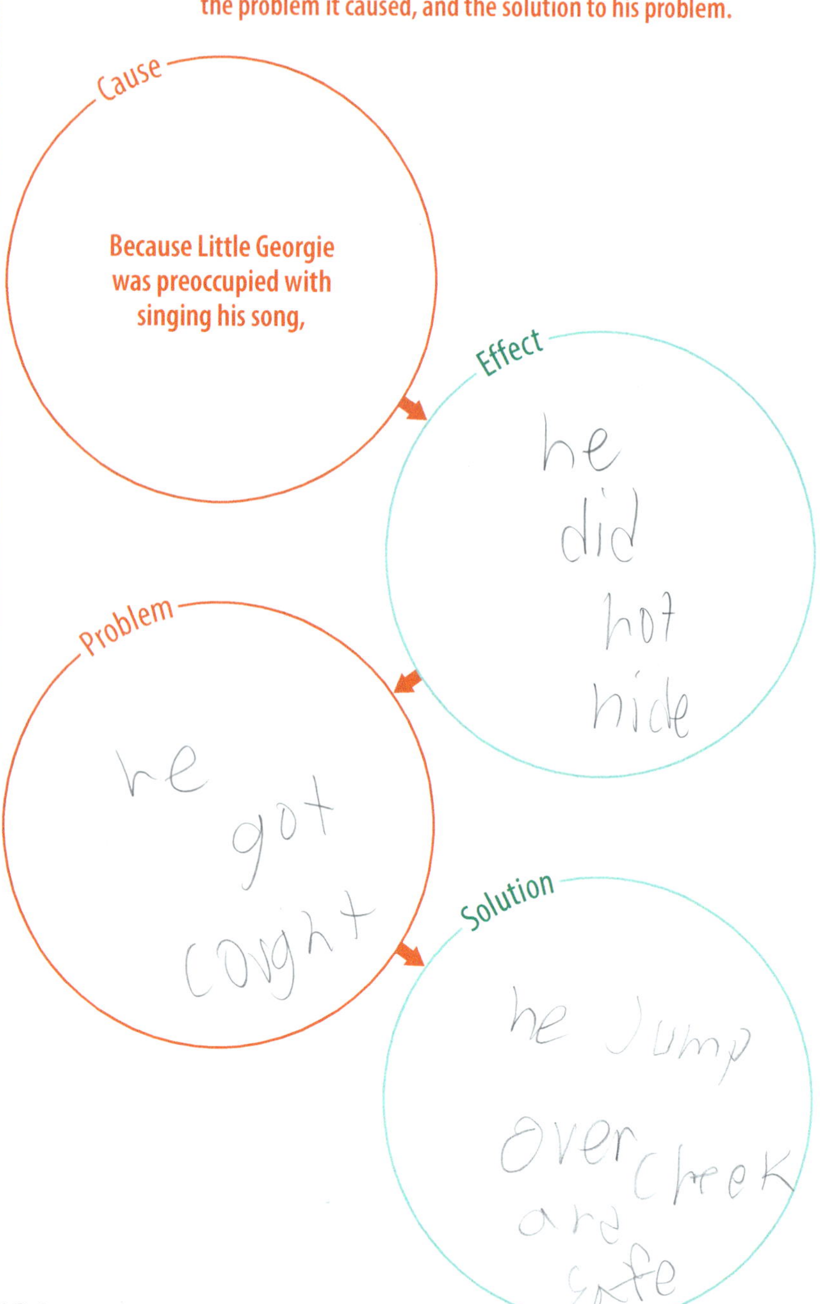

Compare and Contrast Leaders

Complete after "Daniel and the Lions' Den" on page 99.

Compare and contrast the characteristics of the presidents and princes with Daniel.

Presidents and Princes

Both

Daniel

BUILD ON IT

Compare and Contrast Topics

Complete after "Sweet Treats" on page 114.

Fill in the chart below to compare and contrast maple syrup and honey.

Sweet Treats

Topic: maple syrup		Topic: honey
	compare similarities	
	contrast differences	
comes from		comes from
collected using		collected from
the best is		the best is

Describe the Characters

Complete after "A Friend in Sable" on page 167.

Write in the main character and a one-word description about her. In the surrounding circles, write other characters and a one-word description for each.

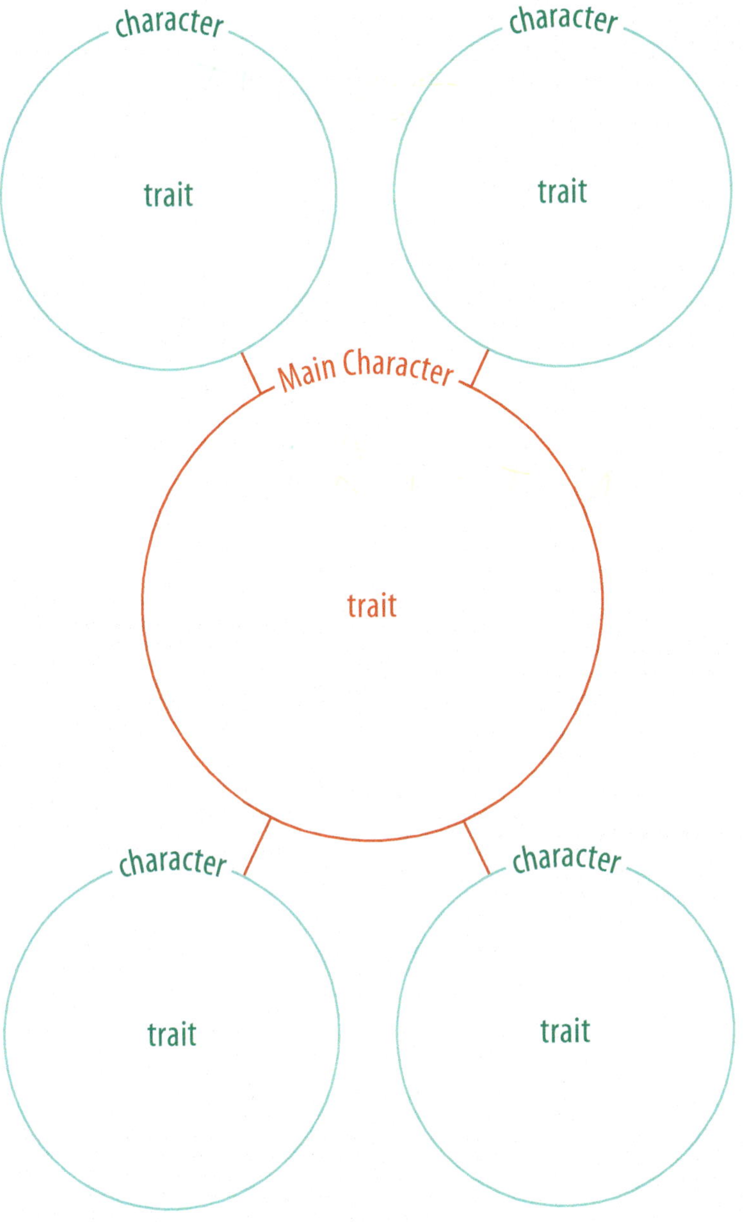

Compare and Contrast Topics

Complete after "Which Is Which?" on page 183.

Write a selection comparing and contrasting your favorite school subjects using the diagram you charted on page 113. Write a paragraph of similarities and a paragraph of differences. You may choose to use some of these signal words:

Word Bank

however both although different similar alike